Children's Christian Education

12 Essentials for Effective Church Ministry to Children and Their Families

BERNARD M. SPOONER, PH.D.
Compiler and General Editor

ROSS WEST
Publishing Consultant and Process Editor

In Collaboration with

JASON CAILLIER, NORMA HEDIN, DIANE LANE, CHRIS LIEBRUM, PHIL MILLER, AND ROYCE ROSE

Christian Leadership Publishing
Coppell, Texas

Children's Christian Education:
12 Essentials for Effective Church Ministry to Children and Their Families

No part of this book may be used or reproduced in any manner whatsoever without written permission, except in the case of brief quotations. For information, contact Christian Leadership Publishing, 330 Spyglass Drive, Coppell, Texas 75019-5430

Bernard M. Spooner, Compiler and General Editor
Ross West, Publishing Consultant and Process Editor

ISBN: 10: 1502403943
ISBN: 13: 9781502403940

Subject Heading: Religious Education

To the staff consultants with whom I
partnered for many years when with Texas
Baptists (the Baptist General Convention
of Texas): Eliseo Aldape, Bill Arnold,
Carl Bozeman, Bob Cavin, Bob Fuston,
Harold Hanson, Diane Lane, Chris Liebrum,
Frank Miller, Phil Miller, Dennis Mitchell,
Bob Oldenburg, Chuck Padilla,
Dennis Parrott, Andre Punch, LaVern Plett,
Hazel Rodgers, Royce Rose, Richard Sims,
Vince Smith, Wil Tanner, Brad Thompson,
Eric Williams, Keith Williams,
Nelda Williams, and Jane Wilson.

Included also in this dedication are
Barbara Prier and the capable and caring
ministry assistants she led.

Contents

Contributors ix

Introduction
By Bernard M. Spooner, Ph.D...xiii

Foreword
Part 1: *By Diane Lane, D.Ed.Min.* xvii

Foreword
Part 2: *By Chris Liebrum, Hon. D.H.*.................................... xxiii

Essential #1
Value the All-Age Bible Teaching Approach of
Sunday School and Small Groups
by Bernard M. Spooner, Ph.D. 1

Essential #2
Ground Children's Ministry on Biblical and
Theological Foundations
by Phil Lineberger, D.Min....21

Essential #3
Understand the Context for Ministry for
Today's Children and Their Families
By Norma S. Hedin, Ph.D. 37

Essential #4
Grasp the Potential for Spiritual Formation for
These Young Children
*By Jason Caillier, M.A. Religious Education
(candidate for Ph.D.)* 49

Essential #5
Develop Skills for Securing Support from the
Pastor, Staff, and Congregation
By Cory Hines, Ph.D. 63

Essential #6
Ensure Quality Teaching for Children
*By Charles Smith, M.A. Religious Education
(candidate for Ed.D.)* 75

Essential #7
Develop Creative Approaches for Reaching and
Attracting Children and Their Families
By Shelly Melia, Ph.D. 95

Essential #8
Provide Appropriate Quality Ministry to
Children and Their Families
By Marcia McQuitty, Ph.D., with Shelly Melia, Ph.D. 109

Essential #9
Lead in Providing Facilities and Equipment for an Attractive
Learning Environment
By B. J. Cranford, M.A. Religious Education 123

CONTENTS

Essential #10
Develop Skills for Securing, Developing, Motivating, and
Ministering to Caring Leaders and Teachers
By Donna B. Peavey, Ph.D. 137

Essential #11
Developing a Viable System for Communicating with Children,
Parents, Teachers, and the Congregation
By Kristi Williams, Ph.D... 151

Essential #12
Motivate Teachers and Parents
by Bernard M. Spooner, Ph.D... 171

**Appendix 1 Additional Facility Considerations for
Education Space for Preschoolers and Children**
By Keith Crouch, AIA, NCARB 189

Appendix 2 Children's Room Diagrams
By B. J. Cranford, M. A. Religious Education........................197

Appendix 3 Teaching Plans
By Dennis Parrott, M.A. Religious Education 201

Notes..217

Contributors

**_Jason Caillier, M.A. Religious Education
(candidate for Ph.D.):_**
assistant professor and director of Master of Family Ministry
degree, Dallas Baptist University, Dallas, Texas

**_B. J. Cranford, M.A. Religious Education
(candidate for Ed.D.):_**
director of administrative services, First Baptist Church,
Keller, Texas, who also served eleven years as minister
of childhood education in the church, with previous service
in churches in Missouri and Oklahoma

Keith Crouch, AIA, NCARB:
director, Church Architecture, Baptist General
Convention of Texas

Norma S. Hedin, Ph.D.:
senior fellow of the Institute, professor of Foundations
of Education, director of master's degree programs, B. H. Carroll
Theological Institute, Arlington, Texas

Cory Hines, Ph.D.:
vice president for graduate affairs, Dallas Baptist University, who
also served churches for a number of years

Diane Lane, D.Ed.Min.:
preschool and children's specialist, Bible Study/Discipleship Center, Baptist General Convention of Texas

Chris Liebrum, Hon. D.H.:
director, Church Ministry Resources, Baptist General Convention of Texas

Phil Lineberger, D.Min.:
pastor, Sugar Land Baptist Church, Sugar Land, Texas; former president of the Baptist General Convention of Texas; frequent curriculum writer for BaptistWay Press®

Marcia McQuitty, Ph.D.:
formerly professor of childhood ministry and director of the childhood Ph.D. program at Southwestern Baptist Theological Seminary, Fort Worth, Texas, semiretired

Shelly Melia, Ph.D.:
assistant professor and director of the Master of Arts in Childhood Ministry degree, Dallas Baptist University; served churches as childhood minister in Florida, Oklahoma, and Texas, most recently the First Baptist Church of Burleson, Texas, for eighteen years

Dennis Parrott, M.A. Religious Education:
formerly director, Bible Study/Discipleship Center, Baptist General Convention of Texas (retired); veteran Christian education leader and consultant; frequent curriculum writer for BaptistWay Press®

Donna Peavey, Ph.D.:
professor of Christian Education, New Orleans Baptist
Theological Seminary, New Orleans, Louisiana; formerly served as
childhood minister in several churches

***Charles Smith, M.A. Religious Education
(candidate for Ed.D.):***
minister of education, First Baptist Church
of Grand Prairie, Texas; longtime children's minister; and
conference leader in Texas and across many states

Bernard M. Spooner, Ph.D.:
distinguished adjunct professor and first dean, Graduate School
of Ministry, Dallas Baptist University, Dallas, Texas; formerly
director of Sunday School/Discipleship Division of the Baptist
General Convention of Texas

Kristi Williams, Ph.D.:
preschool minister, Johnson Ferry Baptist Church,
Marietta, Georgia

Introduction

BY BERNARD M. SPOONER, PH.D.

Why This Book?

This book is a fresh and comprehensive resource of twelve essentials for providing quality Christian education for children (ages six through eleven). It grew out of a concern that pastor, staff, and lay leaders grasp the potential this age group has for gaining concepts about God, the Bible, the church, and the family. This book addresses some important issues that have not always been discussed in recent years, such as:

- Is the all-age Bible teaching plan of the Sunday School viable in today's church?
- What does the Bible say to leaders today about Christian education for children? Does it matter that they are taught?
- How does the context for ministry impact Christian education for children? Is this context leading churches to neglect the potential for helping them get a foundation for biblical faith?
- How can children's ministers get the attention and support of the pastor, staff, and the congregation? Some staff members feel isolated and neglected in their important ministry.

- Does quality teaching matter for this age group? How do we help volunteer teachers see greater value in their ministry of teaching?
- What are churches doing to attract young families with children, and what role do facilities play in providing well for young children?
- How do leaders help teachers and other leaders find fulfillment in ministering to children?
- How can volunteers be appropriately motivated? Do volunteers work for the pastor and staff, or do they have their own call in ministry?

This book is designed for training ministry students at the undergraduate and graduate levels who anticipate serving on the paid vocational church staff. In addition, it is designed to be used by church leaders to train volunteer teachers and workers to conduct Bible teaching and learning for this age group. It provides guidelines for reaching and ministering to children and their families. Also, while it is written from the perspective of people of the Baptist faith tradition, it can also be used to train ministers and lay volunteers teachers in other Evangelical traditions.

The goal has been to provide a resource that is academically sound and yet practical in application. The book will be used as an academic textbook. The content also provides guidelines for developing and conducting teaching and learning for this age group. While the book gives primary focus to Bible teaching for this age group, it also gives guidelines for ministry to the group.

This volume is composed of twelve essentials for doing quality Christian education for the children's age group. Each chapter addresses one of the essentials needed for the most effective Bible teaching ministry for this age group and also gives strong focus to working with the families of children—single-parent families or families with both parents in the home. The final chapter addresses an urgent need for working with volunteers in the church. It empha-sizes servant leadership and a biblical theology that recognizes that all are called to ministry. The pastor and staff have a special and unique role in equipping the lay teachers and leaders. The hope is that a mood of excitement for working with children will be evi-dent in each chapter.

This book is part of a series that provides the essentials for effective church ministry to all age groups, as follows: *Preschool Christian Education; Children's Christian Education; Youth/ Collegiate Christian Education;* and *Adult Christian Education.*

Who Needs This Book?

University and seminary professors will find this volume a good choice as a supplemental textbook for preparing ministers. It will also be a valuable tool for children's ministers, pastors, general staff leaders, and lay leaders in the local churches.

Some Possible Uses of This Book

Among the possible uses of this book are:

- It can be used in university and seminary courses.
- It can be used in ministry student internships in universities and seminaries.
- It can be used for training volunteer teachers and leaders in a retreat setting or over a period of time in regular planning meetings.
- Portions can be used in a parent's meeting.

- A copy of the book can be provided to current teachers and leaders or to new volunteers as they are enlisted. The review questions at the end of each chapter could be used for discussion or copied and used as a suggestion for self-study.

Foreword

PART I

By

Diane Lane, D.Ed.Min.

You are reading this book in order to be equipped on your children's ministry journey. You will continue learning how to reach children and their parents because their relationship with Jesus Christ is the only reason we are in ministry. You are one of the primary spiritual influencers in the child's family.

I grew up in a small country church, Fairview Baptist Church, between Levelland and Sundown, Texas. My mom, Velma May, and the other mothers—Doyce Cooper, Sally Whitaker, Edna Perdue, Susie Henderson, "Bugs" Beadles, Doris Parker, Clemma Wesley, Martha Robbins, Ruth Cone, Doris Parker, and Lois Lucille Kay— took on the responsibility of teaching what was known then as beginners, primaries, juniors, intermediates, and young people. None of them were teachers by trade. They were stay-at-home moms who knew they wanted their children to know God's love. They learned how to teach by reading study course books that the Baptist Sunday School Board produced for training church leaders and teachers. These books told them how to teach, what to say to children and how to say it, and why loving children unconditionally was important. As I reflect on my spiritual heritage, my spiritual foundation is strong because they read books like the one you are reading now.

The people who wrote some of the first books on how to teach preschoolers and children books depended on solid educational values and related those principles to biblical content. I am so glad they did. Robbie Trent, author of *Your Child and God*; Bob and Anna Harty, coauthors of *Made to Grow*; Eugene Chamberlain, author of *When Can a Child Believe*; Muriel Blackwell, author of *Potter and Clay* (still my favorite)—all influenced and set the standard for generations of ministers.

Individuals responsible for curriculum wanted the common person to be able to teach preschoolers and children in the Bible study setting. A few of the pioneers, such as Delores Baker, Elsie Rives, Cosette Baker, Bob Fulbright, Beth Taylor, Bill Young, Florrie Anne Lawton, Ada Rutledge, Sybil Waldrop, Cos Davis, Tommy Sanders, and Mary Ann Bradberry, developed and wrote curriculum clearly in order that every teacher could study the sessions and help every child understand the importance of his or her relationship with God.

Seminary and university professors such as Dr. Anne Bradford, Dr. Jeroline Baker, Hazel Morris, Dr. Marcia McQuitty, and Dr. Tommy Sanders taught us their life philosophy because teaching others about God is the most valuable profession in the world.

Other individuals were great role models who studied, practiced, and lived as Christian examples for us. They took to heart living out God's word because their desire was for their philosophy and their actions to coincide. Influencers with the Baptist General Convention of Texas, such as Melva Cook, Nelda Williams, Karl Bozeman, Bill King, Dennis Parrott, and Dr. Bernie Spooner, long-tenured director of the Sunday School Division of the BGCT, worked to ensure this philosophy would stay strong. Now Phil Miller, Keith Lowry, Jane Wilson, and David Adams are investing their lives so others will know how to reach our world for Christ. Other states have had trailblazers also. The Baptist State Convention of North Carolina had Myra Motley, Hilda Mayo, Bob Goode, Cathy Hopkins, Janice Haywood, and Cheryl Markland. Tennessee Baptist Convention trailblazers included Helen Kennedy, Sammie Meek, Doris Monroe, Liz Lee, Martha Couch, Sue Raley, Vicki Hulsey, and Julie Heath. Louisiana Baptist Convention was fortunate to have Evelyn Henderson, Dan Fowler, Carolle Greene, and David Anderson. Others could be named.

You are now the trailblazers for others. As you live out godly principles and model positive ways to respond to children, you will demonstrate God's unconditional love. As you impact the lives of children and their families, remember Psalm 16:11 (NIV84):

> You have made known to me the path of life;
> you will fill me with joy in your presence,
> with eternal pleasures at your right hand.

Foreword

PART II

By

Chris Liebrum,

Hon. D.H.

The use of the term *Sunday School* is somewhat misleading. Although in most cases Sunday School takes place on Sunday, it can, and for many churches does, take place all through the week. Additionally it is much more than *school*, which implies just an academic pursuit of knowledge. In its truest form, Sunday School can help bring about true discipleship, evangelistically lead people to Christ, and be the mechanism that ministers to people in need. Some have successfully rebranded the term *Sunday School* to communicate a more contemporary feel, but in many cases defining the new terms usually begins with the statement, *You know. It's like Sunday School.* It's just hard to fix something that ain't broke!

The age-graded, church-wide Bible study program called Sunday School has through the years been the proven method to accomplish most of what we read in Matthew 28:19–20, the Great Commission. Here are just a few reasons:

1. It can provide for the entire church family an educational system that will ensure that everyone attending can receive a systematic understanding of the New and Old Testaments. With a fully age-graded approach, you can also ensure that the message of the gospel will be delivered in an age-appropriate manner.

2. Lost attendees can come to know and accept Christ by hearing God's word taught to them over a period of time. The Bible tells us that God's word is powerful enough to draw people into a relationship with Christ (Hebrews 4:12).

3. New Christians can discover weekly what it really means to be a follower of Christ. Discipleship should be a key outcome of a well-prepared Bible study experience.

4. Seasoned believers can continue to allow familiar passages to speak new insights to their lives. I love the phrase from the old classic hymn: "What seems each time I hear it, more wonderfully sweet."[1]

5. The matrix of a church-wide Sunday School system is a wonderful way to communicate to all members the work, mission, and activities of the church. It can also serve as a convenient and systematic way for people to give and to be reminded about their Bible commitment to support the work of the church through their tithe.

As a young minister with both a Baptist university degree and a Baptist seminary degree in hand, it didn't take me long to understand that this thing called church was not something I could do by myself. If I was going to successfully see people come to Christ and have them grow in their faith, I needed the partnership of the laity. Sunday School provides an excellent way to marshal the laity and provide for them a way to live out their calling in a meaningful manner.

Essential #1

VALUE THE ALL-AGE BIBLE TEACHING APPROACH OF SUNDAY SCHOOL AND SMALL GROUPS

by Bernard M. Spooner, Ph.D.

What approach should a church use to reach and disciple people? What kinds of groups are effective? Does the all-age Bible teaching plan of Sunday School have a place in church ministry today? What about home groups?

There are many approaches to and uses for small groups, and there seems to be a consensus that effective discipleship happens in smaller groups.[2] Well-known leaders such as Rick Warren and Bill Hybels have used home groups from the beginning as a means of fellowship and discipleship. Churches of all sizes continue to use small-group Bible study groups such as Sunday School. The focus of this chapter and the book as a whole is on Great Commission–driven Bible study or Bible teaching groups.

Some years ago the Travis Avenue Baptist Church of Fort Worth, Texas, commissioned a study group to review its ministry and to suggest ways to help the church become more effective. (I was fortunate to be involved fully in this experience.) As a part of the process, the team visited fourteen of the largest churches in America. Two people went to each church. The team used an extensive questionnaire to gather an inventory of what these churches did to reach people and do ministry. Some of the things we found were

1. All of these churches had a clear focus on reaching people. Our church also focused on reaching people. However, few results came from our efforts.

2. All of these churches used an all-age Sunday School Bible teaching plan as a strategy for reaching and providing basic discipleship for people in their locations. Our church used this strategy, but we also had numerous other activities every day and night of the week. The numerous activities exhausted the time and energies of our leaders and teachers.

3. All of these churches simplified their ministries to help focus their leaders and members on outreach and evangelism. To get results, most of these churches had limited schedules to protect the time of their leaders. We realized that we needed to simplify our schedule to better focus on our priorities.

4. The pastors of these churches were hands-on leaders and believed that all members were to be mobilized to contribute to reaching out and evangelizing their cities. We realized that we needed to challenge more of our members to become involved in meaningful, focused ministries through our church.

5. All churches had adequate parking for all who attended. We had a serious shortage of parking, and we realized that we must give a priority to adding more parking.

6. Some of these churches gave minimal attention to discipling their people and to missions, however. While we learned much from these churches and significantly changed our scheduling to focus more of our energies on outreach and evangelism, *we did not drop or decrease our discipling ministries.*

Our team summarized the findings of the study, reviewed our church's ministry plan, looked at community demographics, and began to develop a path for the future for our church. It was clear to us that we had our own unique situation to address. We had learned some significant lessons from our study of these great churches, including that the vision for Travis Avenue Baptist Church needed to call for simplifying our ministry and giving more focus to reaching people in our city and in our local community. In light of our own situation, though, we felt that we needed to strengthen missions and discipleship and to give clear priorities to each of these.[3]

> We changed our scheduling to focus more of our energies on outreach and evangelism, but *we did not drop or decrease our discipling ministries.*

> There are few if any wrong ways to reach people when leading them with integrity to faith in Jesus Christ and discipling them in the faith.

Many things have changed in our society since the time of that study. However, one important factor that remains the same is that Bible teaching should always be central to Christian education for children and for all age groups of the church. Bible-based materials are valuable as well. However, for Baptists and most evangelical faith groups, the entire work of ministry and missions gives strong focus to Bible teaching in small groups as the primary strategy of work.

Let me say clearly that I believe there are few if any wrong ways to reach people when leading them with integrity to faith in Jesus Christ and discipling them in the faith—"teaching them to obey everything I have commanded you" (Matthew 28:20, NIV84).[4] Caring Christian people will always seek new and creative ways to reach out whether it is in a historic church in the United States or as missionaries among all kinds of unreached people groups across the world. We should use and support a great variety of approaches for ensuring that Christ's Great Commission (Matt. 28:19–20) continues to go forward in our generation. Thankfully, Christians before us found a way to see that the gospel of Christ got to our generation. It is our responsibility to carry Christ's gospel on to others now and for the coming generations. We are to share the gospel now with our generation and prepare believers to pass it on to future generations.

Keeping this focus firmly in mind, the approach of having all age groups meeting on the church campus continues to be valid. For many years now, most church leaders have recognized the practicality and simplicity of having the whole family in Sunday School Bible study at one time. This approach helps to ensure the availability of volunteer teachers and leaders to conduct a ministry of Bible study, reaching people, and caring, and it allows young parents to be in both worship and small-group Bible study since all age groups meet for Bible study at the same time. In addition, this approach gives Sunday School teachers and workers an opportunity to go to worship before or after they have led or taught in the Bible teaching ministry. On the other hand, if worship is provided to adults while their children are in Bible study, one disadvantage is that people may be less willing to serve as teachers and leaders

4

of children because they will miss the opportunity to be in small-group Bible study with other adults as well as the opportunity to be in the worship service.

Understanding Open Groups and Closed Groups

Gene Mims, an experienced church and denominational leader, has described the concepts of these two basic kinds of groups—open groups and closed groups—as follows:

1. *Open Groups.* "Open groups exist to lead people to faith in the Lord Jesus Christ and to transform them into Christlikeness by engaging them in evangelism, discipleship, fellowship, ministry, and worship. Open groups are small kingdom communities designed to bring believers and unbelievers together in an atmosphere of compassion to share the gospel."[5] Dr. Mims goes on to state that open groups are person centered, lay led, and Bible based. He makes clear that the best content for open groups is Bible study.

2. *Closed Groups.* "Closed groups exist to build kingdom leaders and to equip believers to serve by engaging them in a way that moves them toward spiritual transformation through short-term, self-contained training in an atmosphere of accountability to God and to one another."[6]

Worship services and Sunday School groups are open groups, and both contribute to equipping believers. However, a church should be purposeful in providing closed groups for the specific purpose of training individuals for teaching, evangelism, ministry, or whatever needs the individual and/or the church may want to address.

Comparing Small Groups on and off the Church Campus

Many kinds of groups are needed, depending on the circumstances and opportunities in a church community. The chart "Small-Group Comparisons" attempts to reflect on the issues of small groups both on the church campus and in homes or other off-campus settings. This chart draws from the experience of current practitioners and others who seek the best practices for today. One can look at either list and see both strengths and weaknesses of both approaches. My goal for the chart is that readers will consider the strengths of both approaches and will choose what is the most effective approach for their ministry. Many will choose to use both approaches to some extent.

Small-Group Comparisons

All-Age Bible Study on the Church Campus along with Corporate Worship	Small Groups in Homes or in Other Off–Church Campus Settings
1. Provides for believers and unbelievers	1. Provides for believers and unbelievers
2. Provides a means for building lifelong friendships	2. Provides a means for building lifelong friendships
3. Ensures accountability and support of group members for each other	3. Ensures accountability and support of group members for each other

4. Driven by systematic Bible study. Systematic and appropriate curriculum may be chosen for each age group (Some teachers may resist following the church curriculum plan.)

5. Ensures accountability and support of group members for each other

6. Older, stable groups may focus more heavily on fellowship among themselves with less attention to reaching out to unbelievers or the unreached

7. Pastor and staff give hands-on support and guidance to groups through leadership organization

8. Addresses all stages of life from birth through senior adults

9. Benefits from being scheduled following or prior to Sunday worship (This approach usually contributes to participation in worship also.)

4. Groups study the Bible or other content according to the preferences of the teacher and group (Some groups may resist following the church curriculum plan.)

5. Ensures accountability and support of group members for each other

6. Tendency is toward greater emphasis on relationship development over Bible study

7. Pastor and staff give hands-on support and guidance through leaders

8. Focuses primarily on only one age group—either adults or youth—although children may be present

9. Located in communities closer to unreached persons but must intentionally encourage corporate worship

10. Convenient for family since all may attend Bible study and worship simultaneously

11. Teachers and leaders are available since other family members are in Bible study

12. Class or group leadership usually is easily transferred since they are seen as part of the larger organization

13. Facilities are usually designed for the educational needs of each age group—bed babies to senior adults

14. Allows all age groups to worship at once, with child care provided for young children

15. Communicating about missions, other ministries, stewardship, and other needs of the church and community may be more effective

16. Leaders may focus on Bible teaching, ministry, and fellowship and give less emphasis

10. May meet at night during the week, presenting a problem for parents with young children

11. Because of the schedule, it may be more difficult to secure ongoing leadership

12. Transferring leadership when a teacher or group leader moves away may be difficult unless an assistant has been prepared and is in place as part of the group

13. Space is usually not designed for age-appropriate education

14. Unless groups meet near the church on Sunday mornings, child care may be needed

15. Communicating about missions, other ministries, stewardship, and other needs of the church and community may be more limited

16. Provides a natural means for starting a new church for a new people group, including to reaching language groups or different socioeconomic groups

17. Focus is often on *you come* rather than on reaching outsiders

18. Grading age groups too closely may hinder fellowship beyond a limited age group

19. Classrooms for the various age groups require a financial commitment for construction, maintenance, and utilities

20. Church may be several miles from the homes of some members

21. Meeting in the same location and with the entire church provides a greater opportunity to develop loyalty to the greater mission of the church

22. May tend to rely on the content-driven approach to discipleship to the exclusion of more relational aspects

language groups and people of a different socioeconomic groups

17. Starting Bible studies in apartment groups or similar settings takes Bible study where the people are

18. Fosters intergenerational experiences by providing opportunities to be with people of a wide age group

19. Saves the cost of providing facilities as well as the cost of utilities and maintenance

20. When groups meet in their own neighborhoods, little travel is required

21. Leaders and some members may feel neglected by the church, may become less supportive of the sponsoring church, and may not be involved in corporate worship

22. May tend to rely on a more relational approach to the exclusion of content-driven discipleship

As noted in the comparison chart, Sunday School small groups usually are easily transferable from leader to leader. Home Bible studies are sometime necessary though because of the lack of space or other church circumstances or preferences. However, when the leader or teacher is no longer available, it may not be as easy to transfer the leadership of a home group to another leader. Sometimes the group meets in the leader's home. Also, such groups tend to be unique, with something of their own culture. If possible, such groups need to provide the new leader from within the group itself.

Considering Some Best Practices

To complete this discussion, let's consider some best practices. Ken Hemphill and Bill Taylor have extensive experience in church and denominational leadership. In *Ten Best Practices to Make Your Sunday School Work: Sunday School for a New Century,* they provided a comprehensive definition of Sunday School and a list of best practices.

Hemphill and Taylor define Sunday School as "the foundational strategy in a local church for leading people to faith in the Lord Jesus Christ and for building on-mission Christians through open Bible study groups that engage people in evangelism, discipleship, ministry, fellowship, and worship."[7] This definition includes all of the basic biblical functions of the church and represents all of the basic concepts needed for Great Commission–driven Christian education. It helps to ensure the making of disciples.

Hemphill and Taylor also provide a comprehensive list of ten best practices for doing Sunday School. A separate chapter of the book is given to explain each best practice. Here is their list of ten best practices:

- *Commit to the strategy*—A church should commit to Sunday School as being its foundational strategy for doing the work of the Great Commission. Sunday School should provide proper training, teaching, and knowledge for members to be equipped to spread the gospel of Jesus Christ. Planning and available resources (finances, teachers, workers, etc.) are essential to committing to the strategy.[8]

- *Organize with purpose*—Age-appropriate Sunday School groups help the organization to fulfill the purpose of effective teaching. This process arranges people into appropriate groups so that children, youth, and adults are being ministered to on their levels of learning.[9]

- *Build kingdom leaders*—Enlist and develop leaders who are committed to the purpose of the kingdom of God and to building kingdom leaders. These leaders should see their role as a calling from God to be servant leaders rather than just filling an open position in the church.[10]

- *Develop soul winners*—Members and leaders should be equipped for outreach ministries and to go into homes of individuals in confidence to share God's love.[11]

- *Win the lost*—Proper knowledge of Christ and training help to develop leaders who have a heart for ministry and for sharing the gospel of Christ with the lost. They should have a heart for the lost and a passion to see the lost come to the knowledge of Christ.[12]

- *Assimilate people*—This process brings together people of different backgrounds to represent the body of Christ with the same essential purpose, the desire to see the kingdom of God established on earth.[13]

- *Partner with families*—Bible study groups can provide the proper training and resources for families. Some will teach Bible study groups at church. All family members will be better prepared to teach and disciple their own children, husbands, or wives in their homes.[14]

- *Teach to transform*—Engaging in Bible study groups can provide the necessary teaching and guidance needed to understand biblical principles. It also provides individuals

11

opportunities to develop spiritual relationships with other believers, which can lead to spiritual transformation in daily living and in relationship choices.[15]

- *Mobilize for ministry*—Members should be equipped and available to be involved in ministering to others in need in a variety of settings.[16]

- *Multiply leaders and units*—Members should be exposed to the necessary training and development opportunities to help them explore their leadership potential, to guide them toward the service of Christ, and to support and multiply the mission of spreading the word of God and making disciples of Christ.[17]

Although Robert Raikes usually is credited with beginning the Sunday School movement, perhaps no other person has had as much influence on the Sunday School Bible teaching ministry in evangelical churches as Arthur Flake.[18] He has influenced the approach to Bible study, especially among Baptists, for nearly a century. (Flake's classic book, *Building a Standard Sunday School*, was first published in 1922.)[19] His process for growing a great Bible study ministry clearly reflects the Great Commission of Christ.

Flake was a businessman who came to be highly effective in building Sunday Schools. He applied business principles to go along with his deep commitment for reaching people for Jesus Christ through a Bible teaching ministry. He recognized that God could empower pastors and common men and women through the simple method of an all-age Sunday School that met in connection with the major worship service on Sunday. Eventually, he became a paid Sunday School superintendent and later was chosen to lead Sunday School work on a national level at the Baptist Sunday School Board (now Lifeway Christian Resources) in Nashville, Tennessee.

Arthur Flake's process was based on five principles for Sunday School growth.[20] Although these statements may be phrased differently today, they continue in their influence.

- *Know the possibilities*—The possibilities for the Sunday School include three groups. They are (1) the current members of the Sunday School, (2) church members who are not members of the Sunday School, and (3) prospects or people in the church community who have been identified but are not enrolled in a systematic Bible study. He emphasized the importance of organizing and reaching out to unreached people.

- *Enlarge the organization*—Flake's process continued by adding new groups. He demonstrated that growth comes through starting new teaching units (classes or groups). He observed that existing groups usually reach their maximum size within a few months after they are begun and seldom grow very much after that time. So, to bring about permanent and sustained growth, the organization must be continually expanding by starting new classes or groups.

- *Provide the space*—It's been said that space sets the pattern. What this means is that most churches are limited by the classroom space they have, and their Sunday School is limited by the space available. To have an effective teaching ministry for all age groups, priority must be given to providing the classrooms and equipment needed. Classroom space also should be suited to the needs of each age group and provide for a good teaching environment.

- *Enlist and train the workers*—Once plans have been made for additional space for new teaching units, the enlistment and training of new workers must be given top priority. Jesus instructed the disciples to "ask the Lord of the harvest, therefore, to send out workers into his harvest field" (Matthew 9:38). So, leaders must understand that God helps to provide the workers, and we are to pray to God and lead the congregation to pray for the workers needed.

- *Go after the people*—The final and ongoing step in Flake's process is to begin a concerted and sustained outreach plan

13

to go after the prospects. Consistent efforts must be made to contact and cultivate the prospects for each current unit and each new teaching unit. For best results, all Sunday School workers and the entire congregation should be involved, with the pastor's full support and leadership. Flake recognized that the *combined influence of all age groups reaching out to and/or contacting every member and of prospective families* can bring about an immediate impact on each family with promising results for reaching entire families. Outreach approaches today range from personal contacts to special events and personal visitation. As in Flake's day, the best approaches today continue to be personal contacts and personal invitation.

Statements by Church Leaders about the Value of the All-Age Small-Group Bible Teaching Plan

Here are some statements provided by church leaders who use and advocate the small-group Bible study plan for all age groups in churches:

- *Jay Wolf, pastor, First Baptist Church, Montgomery, Alabama.* Our church's small groups mobilize a vast army of servant leaders who grow into the likeness of Christ as they diligently learn and then teach timeless and transforming biblical truths. Furthermore, our small groups enable us to emulate the rich fellowship prescribed for Christ-followers in Acts 2. Our small groups provide Christ-centered communities where we know each other's names and needs. In this fallen world, we need Jesus, and we need each other! Our Bible Fellowship classes for all ages become a living illustration and incarnation of Christ's healing love for every person who participates.

14

- *Randel Everett, former pastor of First Baptist Church, Midland, Texas (now president of the 21st Century Wilberforce Initiative).* Sunday School is to our church what the skeletal structure is to the body. It connects our church for everything we do. Our best ministry, fellowship, Bible study, and outreach come through our Sunday School. Our outreach activities such as Vacation Bible School, recreational camps, ministry extensions, worship, and evangelistic outreach are promoted and followed up through our Sunday School.
- *Steve Mullen, dean, Mary Crowley School of Christian Ministry, Dallas Baptist University, Dallas, Texas.* Knowing and living by God's word provides nourishment for the soul and a lamp for our pilgrimage. A systematic plan for family Bible study allows the Scriptures to affect the first institution God created in the Garden and allows the family to live in freedom.
- *David Procter, executive pastor, Austin Baptist Church, Austin, Texas.* Sunday School for all ages is a proven strategy we believe in at Austin Baptist Church. Our church was begun in July 2007. We have provided quality Bible teaching for all ages from the very beginning. The first staff members we called focused on age-group leadership for children, youth, and adults. Another church allowed us to use their Sunday School space until we could remodel our own leased space. . . . The response has been overwhelming; families and single adults have poured into our building. Many of them had almost given up finding a church that offered Sunday morning Bible study and worship for the whole family.
- *Phil Miller, director, Bible Study/Discipleship, Baptist General Convention of Texas.* In consulting with churches, the ones who have the most trouble in sustained growth are usually the ones who are not readily prepared to meet the needs of the entire family that wants and/or needs to attend their

church. The use of the all-age Bible teaching plan in Sunday School is a first response, indicating to a seeking world that this church is prepared to address the needs of all family members. . . . The biblical foundation speaks to all ages of the family. So should the church today.

- *Royce A. Rose, director, Logsdon Seminary Program, Dallas-Fort Worth, Texas.* One of the values I adopted early in ministry is: *Everyone needs to be involved in regular Bible study with others.* . . . *A second value is: Everyone needs to be involved in regular Bible study no matter what their age.* Children, from birth on, are learning every day and developing their understanding of God. Sunday School provides a setting where they can learn in an age-appropriate setting, guided by Christian teachers. . . . An all-age, church-based Sunday School ministry offers the opportunity for learning with others and learning fresh insights for faith at every stage in life.

- *Morlee Maynard, professor and director of Christian Education Program, Midwestern Baptist Theological Seminary.* Church families today need the opportunity to participate in Bible study on Sunday mornings or whenever a church can provide such an experience. Due to the demands on people today, we have lost the meaning of going to church together as a family. Both Bible study in age-appropriate groupings and worship as a family in the sanctuary play important roles in discipling parents and children as well as single adults and senior adults. Children need to see and hear their parents and others go to and talk about their Bible study groups. Parents need discipling partners with the Bible study teachers of their children.

- *Bill Gambrell, associate pastor, Education/Program Ministries, Johnson Ferry Baptist Church, Marietta, Georgia.* After sixty-three years of life and Sunday School attendance and thirty-eight years of local church ministry, the Sunday

School remains a vital element in my personal spiritual life and in the life of my local church. Sunday School provides: a place for every member of the family to participate in missions, ministry, evangelism, discipleship, and a systematic, comprehensive, and consistent study of the Bible; an opportunity for teaching doctrine and theology; a platform for evangelism; an environment in which to be loved and known; an opportunity to develop volunteers for ministry and service; and a place for dialogue and discussion about the basics of the faith.

- *Bob Fuston, longtime consultant for the Baptist General Convention of Texas.* Fellowship is a key essential in all age group Bible studies and especially with adults. Acts 2:46 records that "Every day they continued to meet together in the temple courts. They broke bread in their homes and ate together with glad and sincere hearts." *Koinonia*, as translated *fellowship*, relates to community, relationship, sharing, and caring for one another. This is accomplished through fellowship, such as eating together, sharing conversation, and involving class members and prospects in various social activities.

- *Robby Barrett, minister of education, First Baptist Church, Amarillo, Texas.* Sunday School for all age groups is the primary ministry for First Baptist Church of Amarillo to accomplish the Great Commission. Through Sunday School, we reach, teach, witness, share, meet needs, and much more. We invite parents to take primary responsibility for the spiritual development of their children. . . . A Sunday morning schedule for Bible study works best for us. By providing classes for all ages, we encourage adults to use their gifts of teaching with preschoolers, children, students, and other adults, or we free them to attend a Bible study class while knowing their children are not only well cared for but are receiving excellent Bible teaching and application.

- *Duke Jones, associate professor of Church Ministry Studies, Southwest Baptist University, Bolivar, Missouri.* I see tremendous value in all-age Bible teaching within the local church. Small groups provide an intimacy that often cannot be found in a much larger group. I also believe that small groups provide better accountability. Since Christian values are more caught than taught, small groups provide an environment where biblical principles can be both taught and caught. Sunday School provides sound doctrine and theology. Sunday School should also provide practical guidelines and opportunities for putting Christian values into action.

- *David Strawn, minister of education, First Baptist Church, College Station, Texas.* Just as with any complex discipline, Christian theology must be built on basic concepts that are enlarged and expanded. It is absolutely vital that children begin learning Bible stories and Bible thoughts so that as they become adolescents, they can begin to organize and synthesize that information into values that will shape their lives. Then as adolescents move into adulthood, the values that they have developed will begin to be expressed in adult life decisions. . . . Having learners grouped together in similar life stages—preschoolers, children, teens, adults, etc.— facilitates presenting biblical material that is appropriate to each group's developmental level. It also permits the utilization of learning activities that are most appropriate for each of those groups.

- *Doug Powell, associate pastor—minister of education, First Baptist Church, Garland, Texas.* For the past quarter century, I have advocated Bible study across the lifespan, for all ages from birth through senior adulthood. For the following reasons, I believe this is the most effective way to approach age-appropriate Bible study opportunities that lead to biblical discipleship, spiritual growth, and pursuit of the Great Commission. A practical reason is that we now live in a historical era that has seen Christian belief and those who attempt to be faithful followers of Christ marginalized in dramatic ways. Therefore, the need to equip believers as defenders of their faith (1 Timothy 3:15) has become acute at earlier ages than in prior times in American (and perhaps global) history.

Review Questions

1. What are some benefits of an all-age Sunday School as compared to the home Bible study approach?

2. When is it best or necessary to use home groups for Bible teaching?

3. What is meant by "foundational strategy" in the definition of the Sunday School by Hemphill and Taylor?

4. What are three or four common themes from the statements of value given by various leaders in the section "Statements by Church Leaders about the Value of the All-Age Small-Group Bible Teaching Plan"?

For Further Reading

Coggin, James E., and Bernard M. Spooner. *You Can Reach People Now*. Nashville, TN: B&H Publishing Group, 1981.

Flake, Arthur. *Building a Standard Sunday School*. Nashville, TN: Sunday School Board of the Southern Baptist Convention, 1922.

Hemphill, Ken, and Bill Taylor. *Ten Best Practices to Make Your Sunday School Work: Sunday School for a New Century*. Nashville, TN: LifeWay Press, 2001.

Mims, Gene. *The Kingdom Focused Church: A Compelling Image of an Achievable Future*. Nashville, TN: Broadman & Holman, 2003.

Spooner, Bernard M., gen. ed. *Christian Education Leadership: Making Disciples in the 21st Century Church*. Coppell, TX: Christian Leadership Publishing, 2012.

Stetzer, Ed, and Eric Geiger. *Transformational Groups*. Nashville, TN: B&H Publishing Group, 2014.

Warren, Rick. *The Purpose Driven Church: Growth Without Compromising Your Message & Mission*. Grand Rapids MI: Zondervan, 1995.

Essential #2

GROUND CHILDREN'S MINISTRY ON BIBLICAL AND THEOLOGICAL FOUNDATIONS

by Phil Lineberger, D.Min.

Nathaniel Branden states, "Of all the judgments we pass in life, none is as important as the one we pass on ourselves."[21]

Grounding children's ministry on biblical and theological foundations helps children develop a proper judgment on themselves based on the biblical teaching that they are created in the image and after the likeness of God (see Genesis 1:27). They come to understand their ultimate value in God's eyes. They are highly esteemed by God. Branden, quoting D. G. Meyers, writes that "research discloses that high self-esteem is one of the best predictors of personal happiness, whereas low self-esteem correlates with unhappiness."[22]

Grounding children's ministry on biblical and theological foundations provides an opportunity for a child's personal happiness to be based on an understanding of God's love and acceptance of the child. "Research on religiosity suggests that children's self-concepts form alongside the concepts they have of God. Appropriate self-esteem is a by-product of drawing close to God; it is an act of faith grounded on believing a person is valuable to God."[23]

Faith development eventually gives meaning and purpose to the life of the child. Helping the child understand his or her worth to God and others is a vital theological foundation. As James W. Fowler, generally considered the founder of the study of faith development, stated,

> Faith, so Niebuhr and Tillich tell us, is a universal human concern. Prior to our being religious or irreligious, before we come to think of ourselves as Catholics, Protestants, Jews or Muslims, we are already engaged in issues of faith. Whether we become nonbelievers, agnostics or atheists, we are concerned with how to put our lives together and with what will make life worth living. Moreover, we look for something to love that loves us, something to value that gives us value, something to honor and respect that has the power to sustain our being.[24]

What little child has not at some point in life lay down on his or her back on a sunny day, gazing up at the sky and wondering what is behind the sky? This is a question of faith. And answering that question from a biblical and theological perspective is essential to the mission of the church.

Why Is Teaching Young Children Essential to the Mission of the Church?

Likely you have heard someone make this statement: *Christianity is only one generation away from extinction.* I first heard that statement at a statewide evangelism rally some years ago, and I have never forgotten it. Rather, I have used it as motivation to continue teaching Scripture from the cradle to the grave.

When Jesus asked his disciples who people thought he was,

> Simon Peter answered, "You are the Christ, the Son of the living God." Jesus replied, "Blessed are you, Simon son of Jonah, for this was not revealed to you by man, but by my Father in heaven. And I tell you that you are Peter, and on this rock, I will build my church, and the gates of Hades will not overcome it" (Matthew 16:16–18, NIV84).[25]

A building or a life is only as strong as its foundation. The foundation of the church is faith in Jesus as the Christ. Jesus builds his church on this faith—the confession that Jesus is the Christ, the Son of the living God. This teaching about faith is relevant and necessary for the mission of the church from the cradle to the grave.

All faith is not biblical faith. Faith may be directed toward significant others. Faith may be directed toward significant events. Faith may be directed toward significant possessions. Faith may be directed toward significant abilities or talents. In a broad sense, faith is simply that which gives meaning and purpose to life.

This understanding is why it is essential to the mission of the church to enter these faith fields with biblical and theological foundations. Paul wrote in 2 Timothy 3:16–17, "All Scripture is God-breathed and is useful for teaching, rebuking, correcting and training in righteousness, so that the man of God may be thoroughly equipped for every good work."

A biblical and theological foundation involves "teaching, rebuking, correcting and training in righteousness" so that a child grows through the years to "be thoroughly equipped for every good work." Growth is a process that continues to be informed and guided by the "God-breathed" word from the cradle to the grave. Teaching and training children should be based on sound biblical and theological foundations.

The writer of Hebrews echoed this passage in 2 Timothy as he wrote, "For the word of God is living and active. Sharper than any double-edged sword, it penetrates even to dividing soul and spirit, joints and marrow; it judges the thoughts and attitudes of the heart" (Hebrews 4:12).

Failing to confront the many invitations to various sorts of faith in the lives of young children with the gospel is to invite the demise of the New Testament church.

The Old Testament Stresses God's Instructions about Teaching Young Children

In the Old Testament, children were seen as a gift from God. In the beginning God instructed people to "be fruitful and increase in number; fill the earth" (Gen. 1:28).

Children were the central feature in God's promise to bless Abraham and "make [him] a great nation" (Gen. 12:2). As the Lord stated, "I will make you into a great nation and I will bless you; I will make your name great, and you will be a blessing." In the next chapter, the Lord said to Abraham, "I will make your offspring like the dust of the earth, so that if anyone could count the dust, then your offspring could be counted" (Gen. 13:16).

Children had a divine connection. Psalm 127:3 states, "Sons are a heritage from the LORD, children a reward from him." In the next chapter, Psalm 128:3–4 reads, "Your wife will be like a fruitful vine within your house; your sons will be like the olive shoots around your table. Thus is a man blessed who fears the LORD."

Children were to be trained. Proverbs 22:6 promises, "Train a child in the way he should go, and when he is old he will not turn from it." *Training* a child means more than addressing just parts of the child's life, such as biblical knowledge, moral values, or a sense of belonging to the faith community. Rather, as one writer states, "Overlooking the primacy of spirituality develops in effect, a potentially life-long impression that faith involves just parts of the person, but does not really touch who people are, and are continually becoming."[26] The spirituality of the child is the entire essence of how the child views God and how the child relates to God and others as a result of that conception.

Children were to be taught. In Judaism, children were given religious instruction first in the home and then boys beginning at about age seven in the synagogue. As the Mishna, the ancient Jewish writing that codified the oral law, states, "At five years the age is reached for studying the Bible, at ten for studying the Mishna, at thirteen for fulfilling the mitzvoth, at fifteen for studying the Talmud . . ." (Avot 5:21).

For the Old Testament Jew, the day began in the Jewish home with a confession of faith called the *Shema,* from Deuteronomy 6:4, "Hear, O Israel: The LORD our God, the Lord is one." The word *shema* simply means *hear.* Children were members of God's covenant with Israel and thus should learn what the covenant entailed. The instructions continue in Deuteronomy 6:6–9, as follows:

> Love the Lord your God with all your heart and with all your soul and with all your strength. These commandments that I give you today are to be upon your hearts. Impress them on your children. Talk about them when you sit at home and when you walk along the road, when you lie down and when you get up. Tie them as symbols on your hands and bind them on your foreheads. Write them on the doorframes of your houses and on your gates.

The psalmist reminded his readers that they should teach their children about the Lord. As Psalm 78:2–7 states,

> I will open my mouth in parables, I will utter hidden things from of old—what we have heard and known, what our fathers have told us. We will not hide them from their children; we will tell the next generation the praiseworthy

deeds of the LORD, his power, and the wonders he has done. He decreed statutes for Jacob and established the law in Israel, which he commanded our forefathers to teach their children, so the next generation would know them, even the children yet to be born and they in turn would tell their children. Then they would put their trust in God and would not forget his deeds but would keep his commands.

Jesus Points Out the Importance of Young Children

Two passages of Scripture in the New Testament that show the importance of children to Jesus are Matthew 18:1–10 and Mark 10:13–16. Both of these passages point to the relationship of children to the kingdom of God. Matthew 18:1–10 reads,

At that time the disciples came to Jesus and asked, "Who is the greatest in the kingdom of heaven?" He called a little child and had him stand among them. And he said: "I tell you the truth, unless you change and become like little children, you will never enter the kingdom of heaven. Therefore, whoever humbles himself like this child is the greatest in the kingdom of heaven. And whoever welcomes a little child like this in my name welcomes me. But if anyone causes one of these little ones who believe in me to sin, it would be better for him to have a large millstone hung around his neck and to be drowned in the depths of the sea. Woe to the world because of the things that cause people to sin! Such things must come, but woe to the man through whom they come! If your hand or your foot causes you to sin, cut it off and throw it away. It is better for you to enter life maimed or crippled than to have two hands or two feet and be thrown into eternal fire. And if your eye causes you to sin, gouge it out and throw it away. It is better for you to enter life with one eye than to have two eyes and be thrown into the fire of hell. See that you do not look down on one of these little ones. For I tell you that their angels in heaven always see the face of my Father in heaven."

Mark 10:13–16 further emphasizes the importance of children in Jesus' eyes:

People were bringing little children to Jesus to have him touch them, but the disciples rebuked them. When Jesus saw this, he was indignant. He said to them, "Let the little children come to me, and do not hinder them, for the kingdom of God belongs to such as these. I tell you the truth, anyone who will not receive the kingdom of God like a little child will never enter it." And he took the children in his arms, put his hands on them and blessed them.

According to Mark 10:14, Jesus became "indignant" at his disciples for trying to keep children from him. The word translated "indignant" can also be translated *angry*. This word describing Jesus' response suggests the seriousness of attempting to exclude little children from coming to him. Excluding little children from coming to Jesus could entail pushing them away or not inviting them. While very few today would push little children away from Jesus, they might keep children from Jesus by not inviting them or teaching and training them.

Judith M. Gundry-Volf, a scholar writing on the topic of children in early Christianity, notes that when Jesus "takes the little children in His arms, lays his hands on them and blesses them, he is teaching that 'the reign of God belongs to children.'"[27] Gundry-Volf also says, "It is probably correct to say that the children's vulnerability and powerlessness seem to lie at the heart of Jesus' extension of the reign of God to them."[28]

Not only did Jesus welcome the little children, but he also told the disciples (the adults) that unless they became like little children they could not enter the kingdom of heaven. What did Jesus mean? It appears that Jesus was saying that it takes a childlike faith to become his trusting follower. The trusting faith of a child that causes the child to learn from the one the child trusts makes the child more likely to enter the kingdom of God.

When Jesus taught that true greatness comes from welcoming and serving little children, he placed the little children right in the center of the church's attention as objects of love, service, and teaching. Mark 9:33–37 tells of another encounter of Jesus with children:

> They came to Capernaum. When he was in the house, he asked them, "What were you arguing about on the road?" But they kept quiet because on the way they had argued about who was the greatest. Sitting down, Jesus called the Twelve and said, "If anyone wants to be first, he must be the very last, and the servant of all." He took a little child and had him stand among them. Taking him in his arms, he said to them, "Whoever welcomes one of these little children in my name welcomes me; and whoever welcomes me does not welcome me but the one who sent me."

The word translated "welcomes" (*dechomai*) in this passage is used especially for hospitality to guests, which implies serving them. Luke 10:8 uses the same Greek word (*dechomai*)—"'When you enter a town and are welcomed, eat what is set before you." Luke 16:4 also uses the same Greek word: "I know what I'll do so that, when I lose my job here, people will welcome me into their houses."[29] To be great in the kingdom of God, disciples are taught to love and serve little children. Gundry-Volf observes, "The teaching is, of course, ironic, for children occupied the lowest rung on the social ladder, and caring for children was a low status activity."[30]

According to the teaching of Jesus, welcoming little children is actually a way of welcoming Jesus and the God who sent him. Conversely, not welcoming little children is a way of rejecting Jesus and the God who sent him.

Not only were little children to be welcomed and served, but they also were to be recognized for their knowledge of Jesus. Matthew 21:14–16 records,

> The blind and the lame came to him at the temple, and he healed them. But when the chief priests and the teachers of the law saw the wonderful things he did and the children shouting in the temple area, "Hosanna to the Son of David," they were indignant. "Do you hear what these children are saying?" they asked him. "Yes," replied Jesus, "have you never read, 'From the lips of children and infants you have ordained praise'?"

Children often have insights about God and Jesus that confound adults. Matthew's account of Jesus' visit to the temple shows the prophetic recognition of Jesus by the little children in contrast to the skepticism and unbelief of the chief priests and scribes. Jesus said that God has "ordained" praise from the lips of children. These insights are God-given and should be accepted as such by those who teach children. They should be applauded and built on with biblical teachings.

Children are special objects of divine care and protection and must not be offended. Jesus offered a stark illustration of how serious an offense it would be to cause a little child to stumble by saying, "But if anyone causes one of these little ones who believe in me to sin, it would be better for him to have a large millstone hung around his neck and be drowned in the depths of the sea" (Matthew 18:6).

Paul Stresses the Importance of Teaching Children in the Home

In Ephesians 6:4, Paul encouraged fathers to bring their children up "in the training and instruction of the Lord." This instruction surely would apply to both parents. In Colossians 3:20–21, Paul wrote, "Children, obey your parents in everything, for this pleases the Lord. Fathers, do not embitter your children, or they will become discouraged."

The father's primary goal in the home was to educate and train his children to understand and obey the biblical teachings. Bible scholar Andrew Lincoln, in commenting on Paul's instruction to fathers in Ephesians 6:4, wrote that fathers were to "teach their children the apostolic tradition about Christ and help to shape their lives in accordance with it."[31]

The father was to educate and train in a loving and patient manner so that the children did not lose heart or give up on learning and practicing these biblical teachings. What was true for the father should be true of anyone who teaches and trains young children in biblical and theological material.

Children were exhorted to obey their "parents in the Lord" (Ephesians 6:1). That is, they were to obey their parents in the context of the biblical teachings and their parents' relationship to the Lord. Obedience is important as a foundational principle for young children because the Scriptures teach us that there is an inherent struggle going on between good and evil in the life of every person.

Genesis 8:21, referring to the situation after the Flood, states, "The LORD smelled the pleasing aroma and said in his heart: 'Never again will I curse the ground because of man, even though every inclination of his heart is evil from childhood. And never again will I destroy all living creatures, as I have done.'"

The writer of Proverbs said, "Folly is bound up in the heart of a child" (Proverbs 22:15). Paul reiterated in the New Testament Book of Romans that "there is no one righteous, not even one" (Romans 3:10). These are important truths to be taught and learned because young people are more easily formed than adults, and it is easier but more crucial to put them on the right path early.

In fact, in order to be considered for the leadership positions of overseer or deacon in a New Testament church, the father was to be judged according to his faithfulness in training his children in the Scriptures. Speaking of the overseer, "He must manage his own family well and see that his children obey him with proper respect. (If anyone does not know how to manage his own family, how can he take care of God's church?)" (1 Timothy 3:4–5). In addition, 1 Timothy 3:12 states, "A deacon must be the husband of but one wife and must manage his children and his household well." Further, Titus 1:6 instructs, "An elder must be blameless, the husband of but one wife, a man whose children believe and are not open to the charge of being wild and disobedient."

What Are Some Scriptural Implications of This Essential?

There are a number of significant implications for the twenty-first-century church for grounding children's ministry on biblical and theological foundations. *The basic implication for grounding children's ministry on biblical and theological foundations is that all children are gifts from God* and should be treated accordingly. In Genesis 30:20, Leah, Jacob's first wife, saw her son Zebulun as a gift from God. "Then Leah said, 'God has presented me with a precious gift. This time my husband will treat me with honor, because I have borne him six sons.' So she named him Zebulun."

Children are not only gifts to parents but also gifts to the church and to the community. As they grow up, they will play varied and significant roles in both church and community. For these gifts to be celebrated and enjoyed, children need the attention and training of the church and community so they will develop a firm biblical and theological foundation.

31

Since children are seen as gifts of joy, churches could benefit by including children in various types of public worship services. Doing this would not only add to the joy and vitality of the churches but could also serve to develop the child's understanding of the biblical and theological foundations of the worship services.

A second implication is that the Scriptures teach us that all people are created in the image and likeness of God. Genesis 1:26 states, "Then God said, 'Let us make man in our image, in our likeness, and let them rule over the fish of the sea and the birds of the air, over the livestock, over all the earth, and over all the creatures that move along the ground.'"

This creative touch from God sets children above every other created thing in terms of the ability to think, reason, and reflect. This creative touch from God not only provides children with inherent worth but also gives them the capacity to respond to biblical teachings and to the guidance of God's Spirit.

Because children are created with the ability to think, reason, and reflect, regular and systematic teaching is important for building a biblical and theological foundation. The writers of the Old Testament understood this as they instructed the people to begin every morning with the *Shema* (see Deut. 6:4) and to heed God's commandments.

A third implication is that churches should work closely with families in the faith development of children. This should include providing solid biblical materials and opportunities for parents to be trained in using these materials. There should be a coordinated effort by the church to keep the parents informed about what their children are being taught each week. By doing this, parents can speak to their children regularly about moral and spiritual matters.

Since children are capable of expressing faith in others, that faith should be nurtured and guided by biblical teachings. As children develop, they need instruction and guidance. They are on their way to becoming adults and need the help of teachers to know what is right and just and what is expected of them as they mature.

Proverbs 22:6 reminds us, "Train a child in the way he should go, and when he is old he will not turn from it." Again, Proverbs states, "My son, do not forget my teaching, but keep my commands in your heart, for they will prolong your life for many years and bring you prosperity" (Proverbs 3:1–2).

A fourth implication is that children should be taught to love Jesus and to never be turned away from Jesus. In Matthew 19:14, "Jesus said, 'Let the little children come to me, and do not hinder them, for the kingdom of heaven belongs to such as these.'"

People who teach and train children should always be reminded that Jesus equated welcoming a little child with welcoming him and the One who sent him. Matthew 18:2–5 records that Jesus

> . . . called a little child and had him stand among them. And he said: "I tell you the truth, unless you change and become like little children, you will never enter the kingdom of heaven. Therefore, whoever humbles himself like this child is the greatest in the kingdom of heaven. And whoever welcomes a little child like this in my name welcomes me."

Further, those who teach children in the church should also be aware that adults can learn important spiritual truths from children. When Jesus told his disciples that an adult who wanted to enter the kingdom of heaven must come as a little child, Jesus was giving them a hint of their need to recover a childlike spirit. Recovering a childlike spirit comes first from observing the spiritual behavior of young children. "Friederich Schleiermacher, the Nineteenth Century Protestant theologian, emphasized that adults who want to enter the kingdom of God need to recover a childlike spirit. For him, this childlike spirit has many components that can be learned from children, such as 'living fully in the present moment' or being able to forgive others and to be flexible."[32]

The spiritual insights that children bring out should be encouraged and guided by biblical teachings. One of the ways of encouraging the spiritual insights of a young person is to involve him or her in some capacity in the service and ministry of the church in age-appropriate ways. God set the example by appointing a young boy named Samuel to serve him. First Samuel 2:18 records, "But Samuel was ministering before the LORD—a boy wearing a linen ephod." Since God trusted a young boy to help in religious service, we should use that example in encouraging young children in the ministry of the church.

It is clear from Scripture that what is taught to children becomes a foundation on which they build. Along with the commitment to remember God and God's commandments, the Hebrew people were reminded to teach the next generations about God's faithfulness.

These biblical teachings were to become a foundation on which children could rely as they grew older. Just as teaching children from a biblical and theological perspective was essential to the life and work of the Hebrew people, so is teaching children from a biblical and theological perspective essential to the mission of the church.

Review Questions

1. How can churches welcome children, contribute to their education and training, and help them mature in the Christian faith?

2. How do churches fall into the trap of teaching only a part of the child?

3. What can a teacher do to help a parent of the child build a biblical and theological foundation in their child?

4. How does a teacher listen for profound spiritual truths from children?

5. How does a teacher model "living in the moment" for the child?

For Further Reading

Anthony, Michael J. *Introducing Christian Education*. Grand Rapids, MI: Baker Academic, 2001.

Branden, Nathaniel. *The Six Pillars of Self-Esteem*. New York: Bantam Books, 1994.

Bunge, Marcia J., ed. *The Child in Christian Thought*. Grand Rapids, MI: William B. Eerdmans, 2001.

Fowler, James W. *Stages of Faith: The Psychology of Human Development and the Quest for Meaning*. New York: HarperCollins, 1981.

Ratcliff, Donald, ed. *Children's Spirituality*. Eugene, OR: Cascade Books, 2004.

Essential #3

UNDERSTAND THE CONTEXT FOR MINISTRY FOR TODAY'S CHILDREN AND THEIR FAMILIES

By Norma S. Hedin, Ph.D.

What is the context for ministry to children and their families today? How do aspects of society and the current context of church ministry affect approaches to ministry to children?

One statistic often quoted is that over one half of individuals who come to faith in Christ do so before the age of twelve. However, long before the age of twelve, children have begun to form religious beliefs.

Who are these young children who enter the doors of our churches with eyes and ears open to the teachings of Scripture? Who are the children who absorb the changeless truths of God's work in the world? What are the contextual factors that affect children and their families today?

Changing demographics, changing families, and changing churches confront the minister who seeks to work with children in the church. The following will explore some of these changes that form the context for ministry to today's children and their families.

Demographics

The number of children in the United States population ages zero to seventeen was at an all-time high in 1960, consisting of 36 percent of the total population. A steady decline has occurred, with the percentage of children ages zero to seventeen in the population in 2012 at 23.5 percent.[33] Of the 73.6 million of all children in this age range, around 24 million of those are ages zero to five, and 24.6 million are ages six to eleven.[34] Almost 50 million of them—more than the population of most countries—are growing, learning, and ready to hear the gospel.

These children come in all shapes and sizes, ethnicities, and socioeconomic backgrounds. The basic changes in demographics in America are reflected in children and their families. The decline in white, non-Hispanic children and the increases in Hispanic and Asian children mirror the overall demographics of the changing population of the United States. The numbers of black children have remained about the same.[35] Diversity is a part of life for children today. More so than any other age group, children fail to notice these differences. However, churches should value the unique perspectives of various ethnic groups and consider those in making decisions about ministry.

The sheer numbers of children in America bring forward other realities. Information from the Kids Count Data Center indicated that in 2012 around 22 percent of children of all ages were in households that were described as *food insecure*. Those under the age of eight in poverty in 2012 were around 48 percent. Issues of poverty and hunger are the everyday experience of many children and their families. While most of the children who attend our churches may not be suffering in this way, this is the reality of many children, and ministers should be aware of the realities in order to minister to those in need.

In terms of family structure, only 64 percent of children ages zero to seventeen lived with two married parents in 2012, down from 77 percent in 1980.[36] While divorce and remarriage do not have the stigma once associated with them, changing family structures do create new dynamics from previous years of ministry with children. Some live in single-parent households, and there are increasing numbers of children living with adults who live together but are not married. So children come to church with different experiences related to family and child-care arrangements.

Education

Children spend a significant amount of time in the classroom. And Americans spend lots of money on education. Public school systems throughout America spent more than $632 billion on elementary and secondary education in 2010–2011. Even with the billions being poured into public education, parents are conflicted about choosing public school systems for their children and report concerns about safety and violence.[37] Educational improvements have led to somewhat higher achievement, but US children still fall behind some other nations in achievement in some areas, particularly in math. America has been described as being in the "middle of the pack" academically and basically "running in place," in terms of progress compared to other nations.[38]

Technology Use

Technology is ever present in families today, and concern with the overuse of electronic media, including television, computers, and electronic games, has led to increased research in these areas. The *ScienceDaily* reported that the sedentary nature of using electronics is associated with adverse health outcomes, including higher BMI (body mass index, a measure of body fat) for children at age seven, higher levels of emotional problems, and poor family functioning.[39] However, some of these effects can be mediated by parental monitoring, and so use of electronics is not always negative. Related to this study are the Child Health Data studies that report that over half of children age six to seventeen have a television in their bedroom, which would be more difficult for parents to monitor.[40]

One concern related to technology use is the debate about whether technology is affecting children's creativity. A recent study building on research in children's creativity for more than fifty years found that "since 1990, even as IQ scores have risen, creative thinking scores have significantly decreased. The decrease for kindergartners through third graders was most significant."[41] The decline in creativity is thought to be due at least in part to the decline of free play.[42] The argument is that since children interact with only a representation of the real world, they are losing the full hands-on experience necessary for brain development. In addition, using technology to distract and soothe an upset child may rob the child of learning how to develop inner resilience and social skills. Not surprisingly, parents and educators disagree about these findings, and a recent blog post created a rousing discussion related to the use of technology for children of all ages.[43] These conversations and studies will need to be explored more fully in the future. Use of technology in the church for teaching children will be part of this discussion.

Health and Physical Development

Medical and health care advances have reduced infant mortality, particularly mortality of preterm babies, and other medical treatments and immunizations have practically eliminated some formerly fatal childhood diseases. However, other challenges have presented themselves for children today.

One concerning trend is the issue of childhood obesity. Statistics vary, but 18 percent or roughly one-fifth of children in America are categorized as obese.[44] Of those ten to seventeen years old, more than 31 percent are categorized as overweight or obese.[45] However, this is not only an American problem, as obesity rates are climbing all over the world.[46] Lack of activity, obsession with technology, lack of safety for outdoor play, and fast food may be contributing to this epidemic.

Other possible concerns relate to increased rates of diagnoses of attention deficit disorder, autism spectrum disorders, and mental health issues among children. Studies have found that in any given year, one out of five children suffers some type of mental disorder.[47] Whether these disorders are the result of family situations or biological realities, some children live with them, and these children come to our churches. Acknowledging these very real struggles and supporting families is critical.

Another serious concern is the increased sexual activity among younger teens and preteens. The University of Texas Health Science Center reports that middle school children as young as twelve are participating in sexual activity.[48] Apart from the moral, emotional, and spiritual aspects of premature sexual activity, the introduction of sexually transmitted diseases at a young age is a concerning health risk. Substance abuse, whether tobacco, drugs, or alcohol, affects some children, as well as violence from crime, bullying, or gang activities. As children age, their exposure to these situations increases, with the accompanying consequences.

While the majority of children and their families in the church may not be impacted by these types of statistics, the reports do alert us to the reality of ministry to children and their families. Most will not live in poverty (depending on your church's context), but some may not reveal their dire situations. Most will not be victims of violence, but children today live in more fear than in earlier years, partially due to their parent's concerns about safety.

George Barna, in his discussion about statistics on child issues, concluded:

> Most of our young people will not end up as alcoholics or drug addicts, but most of them will abuse those substances on an irregular basis and will have one or more close friends who are serious substance abusers. Fortunately, most children will never be the victims of a serious physical crime, but most of them will experience daily fear and scheduling limitations as a result of the growing instances of juvenile violence. Fewer than 20 percent of kids will drop out of school before receiving a high school diploma, but the bigger danger may be their lack of desire to learn or their disinterest in personal excellence. Relatively few youngsters will be physically abandoned by their parents, but millions will be traumatized by receiving their parents' emotional leftovers, as well as by the divorce, separation or adulterous activities that will shatter their family unity. The majority of America's kids are not clamoring for X-rated, profane and violent content on TV or movies and video games, but they are constantly seduced and tantalized by messages and imagery that blur or overstep the boundaries of decency. Maybe our young ones are not sexually depraved beings that some have charged, but we must recognize that their perceptions of sexual propriety have been sufficiently compromised and that most kids will wind up with a sexually transmitted disease and an unfulfillable longing to return to virgin status.[49]

Awareness of the context in which our children and their parents live will help the church support families in their efforts to develop the spiritual foundations that help children to know God and lead holy lives.

Church Context

Change is reflected in church ministry as well as in society. Due to some of the societal issues noted, churches incorporate a variety of safety procedures designed to protect children from harm. Background checks on workers, playground equipment with safety features, and secure rooms with fire alert systems are common.

Churches should have a vested interest in the spiritual condition of children and their families. Most churches provide children's ministries, including designated facilities, equipment, curriculum, and resources. In addition, many churches provide weekday programs, special programs such as Vacation Bible School, AWANAs, field trips, summer camps, and even academies.

However, ministry to children is not necessarily a top priority for churches. Barna conducted a study of leading Protestant churches and found that only 24 percent identified ministry to children as a priority. Related to this was the low budget assigned to children's ministry, along with the attitude toward qualifications for children's ministers, which revealed the persistent attitude that hiring a staff member to work with children is a low priority.[50] Barna described a disturbing finding in his research:

> . . . church leaders often view the children's ministry as a "loss leader"—a retail term used to describe the marketing of a product that loses money but generates a sufficient payback through ancillary benefits. Children's ministries are frequently marketed to adults because research shows that millions of parents want their children to have a positive church experience and that they will attend any nearby church that provides their children with a consistently high-quality ministry. Viewed from that angle, many churches do not adequately or appropriately support ministry to children because kids are seen as the "bait" that enables the church

to land the real treasure—i.e., adults—rather than as a valuable, if unrefined, treasure in themselves.[51]

While ministry to children and their families may not be the primary emphasis of a congregation, it should be one of the most important ministries for the future of the church and for the growth of the church. In the Fact2000 Study, sponsored by Faith Communities Today, their results revealed that evangelical Protestant congregations tended to have more young adults and families with children than other participants in the study.[52] Key indicators of growth for congregations at that time also revealed that involving children in worship and attracting young adults and families with children were important to the growth of congregations.[53] Additionally, research on megachurches also supports the need to appeal to young adults and families. "Megachurches are not just filled with adults but with vast numbers of children and teens as well."[54]

The good news is that as some young adults have children, they begin to think about returning to church. Some of these young adults may not have attended church for some time. About one-sixth of parents (17 percent) reported that having a child helped them reconnect with church after a long period of not attending. Another one-fifth (20 percent) said they were already active but became more involved after having children.[55]

One current emphasis in church ministry to preschoolers and children is the partnership between parents and the church "in the mutual effort to raise God-loving and God-fearing children."[56] Barna's research ultimately led to his prescription for raising "spiritual champions," which is "the acknowledgement that the spiritual development of children is first and foremost the responsibility of parents and that a church is best poised to assist rather than lead in that process."[57]

Janice Haywood, a respected leader in church ministry to preschoolers and children, agrees. In *Enduring Connections: Creating a Preschool and Children's Ministry,* she proposes that increasing numbers of ministers and laypeople are recognizing the importance of ministry to children as it relates to the health of the church. She states:

- Parents value their children. Not only do they want the "very best" for their children, but they seek assistance and encouragement in their parental role.
- Ministers recognize that an effective, safe childhood ministry attracts young families.
- Churches understand that faith is built most effectively from childhood, and strong churches can help build strong spiritual foundations.
- Insightful parents, ministers, and church leadership acknowledge that if the church is to impact our pagan world with the hopeful gospel message, we must begin with children.[58]

She also supports the idea that ministry to children is rooted in ministry to families, and that congregations must have the core values of seeking to "successfully connect children to God, children and parents to a community of faith, and childhood ministry to the mission and/or vision of the congregation."[59]

While not proposing to totally do away with age-graded experiences, family ministry proponents are concerned that children do not have appropriate opportunities to observe the next stage of development that may draw them forward to help them grow in their faith or to see how their parents or adults express their faith through worship. Primarily, those who focus on family ministry are concerned that churches send the incorrect message that the church provides spiritual teaching and the parents' role is just to bring them to church.[60]

Those who teach and write in children's ministry have identified several approaches to the spiritual formation of children, each of which provides a different perspective for the church. Four of these models of children's spiritual formation are presented in *Perspectives on Children's Spiritual Formation*,[61] edited by Michael Anthony. The four models include:

> *Contemplative-Reflective* believes that Christian spirituality must go beyond the simple transmission of biblical information and include active pursuit of an intimate relationship with God. As a result, the emphasis is on contemplative prayer and awareness of the Spirit.

> *Instructional-Analytic* has a high regard for cognitive thought process and focuses on consistent and systematic study of God's word. As a result, it is characterized by a systematic presentation of biblical teaching and emphasis on Scripture memory. Churches utilizing this model use programs like AWANAs and curriculum focused on content and Bible memory.

> *Pragmatic-Participatory* focuses on active learning and enjoyable learning activities. As a result, the activities include dramatic presentations of Bible stories, choreographed singing, numerous activities, and integration of instructional technology. Megachurches often use this type of approach.

> *Media-Driven Active-Engagement* models high-energy programs where children are always moving and creatively expressing themselves through music, drama, and activities. Role plays, active games, technology, and interactive movement are used in these models.

Those who minister to children must work with the church, the pastoral staff, and the workers to identify which approach best articulates the theology and philosophy of children's ministry for their congregation. These decisions are inextricably tied to the vision and mission of the congregation.

The following chapters will explore the practical aspects of ministry to children. The focus of this chapter has been to create awareness of the context of this ministry—the descriptions of the children in this generation who will come to our churches with their unique backgrounds.

Review Questions

1. How would you describe the children in your church's ministry? What are the family situations and needs of children in your congregation?

2. What children's health needs are present in your church? What percentage of the children in your congregation have emotional or mental challenges?

3. How are the parents in your congregation handling technology for their children?

4. Of the four models of children's spiritual formation, which best describes your church's approach? What aspects of the mission or vision connect to this decision?

For Further Reading

Anthony, Michael J. *Perspectives on Children's Spiritual Formation: 4 Views*. Nashville, TN: B&H Academic, 2006.

Barna, George. *Transforming Children into Spiritual Champions.* Ventura, CA: Regal Books, 2003.

Haywood, Janice. *Enduring Connections: Creating a Preschool and Children's Ministry.* St. Louis, MO: Chalice Press, 2007.

Essential #4

GRASP THE POTENTIAL FOR SPIRITUAL FORMATION FOR THESE YOUNG CHILDREN

By Jason Caillier, M.A. Religious Education (candidate for Ph.D.)

"Who do you think is the most important person in the whole Bible?" It sounds like a question a children's Bible study teacher may pose to a classroom full of kids. Instead, that is the question my seven-year-old son posed to me one night as I was putting him to bed. Of course, part of the purpose behind his question might have been to delay bedtime, but I am a firm believer in the holy moments that occur when we lay our head down on the pillow and begin to contemplate questions that are bigger than ourselves. I like to call these moments *bedtime theology*. Now, I could have answered the question simply and moved along, but instead we had an awesome conversation about Jesus.

That was not the first time my son and I conversed about some deep spiritual realities from God's word. In fact, it was not the first time he was the one who brought up a spiritual topic. Young children are thinking about God in ways that adults often are not aware. As we teach children in our churches, we expect them to answer questions about spiritual matters because we have couched our time with them in a structured way that leads toward those topics. However, children also experience and think about the reality of God throughout their daily lives. God is pursuing a love relationship with all people throughout all of their lives. As children become more aware of the world around them, they also are becoming more aware of the love God has for them. It is a privilege we hold to be able to teach children the revealed truths of God found in Scripture. The importance of this privilege comes with the great responsibility to equip ourselves to understand children.

Leaders of children's ministries build ministries based on what they believe are the capabilities and spiritual potential of children. For church leaders who do not believe children have the ability to genuinely understand spiritual things or have a connection with God, the ministries to children often become moments of Bible study mixed with child care. Leaders who believe the children are becoming aware of the realities of God and God's love for them build ministries that lay the foundation for children to have a genuine relationship with God. Furthermore, leaders who believe children can have encounters with God while they are young provide opportunities and create environments for children to worship, pray, and connect with God.

So the questions to be considered include the following: Do you believe children are able to have experiences that contribute to their spiritual development? Do you believe parents and ministry leaders—empowered by the Holy Spirit—are able to help lay a foundation in the life of a child that will have significant bearing on a lifetime, and eternity, of spiritual connection to God for the child? This book as a whole and this chapter specifically seeks to help you understand the potential for spiritual formation in the childhood years.

The Potential for Spiritual Formation in Children Expressed in Scripture

A brief look at Scripture provides a foundation for understanding the responsibility of parents and the church to help children connect with God and the potential of a child to grow spiritually. In Deuteronomy 6, Moses gathered the people of Israel to deliver a message from God saying that the statutes and commandments of God were to be taught to children by their parents and the community of faith. Deuteronomy 6:7 expresses this directive in the phrase "teach them diligently to your children" (RSV). In Ephesians 6:4, Paul encouraged fathers to bring their children "up in the discipline and instruction of the Lord" (NASB). Both of these verses reveal that there is a precedent established by God for teaching spiritually significant matters to children. Not only is it a precedent worthy of emulation, but particularly in the case of the passage in Deuteronomy, teaching and instructing children in the way of the Lord shaped aspects of daily living and the passing of cultural expressions from one generation to the next.

In seeking to determine the potential a child has to grow spiritually, the early life of Jesus gives some clues. While comparatively little is written in the Bible about this stage of Jesus' life, the final verse of Luke 2 gives much insight. "And Jesus increased in wisdom and stature, and in favor with God and men" (Luke 2:42, NASB). This verse encapsulates three ways in which modern science examines the development of children and adds the fourth dimension of spiritual development. Jesus' increase in wisdom is comparative to cognitive development, his increase in stature is comparative to physical development, his increase in favor with God is comparative to spiritual development, and his increase in favor with people is comparative to social and emotional development.

51

Scripture seems to suggest that in the humanity of Jesus there was a process of growing in all of these areas including his spiritual growth. While Luke 2:42 is in reference to Jesus at twelve years old, Luke 2:40 speaks of Jesus' growth since infancy. In his commentary, *The Gospel of Luke*, Joel B. Green (1997) states that Jesus as a child "already possessed the qualities that will make him extraordinary in later life." [62] While it would seem possessing those qualities from infancy would be obvious for the Son of God, it is important to note that Scripture says these qualities were *increasing* toward their full expression (see Luke 2:42, NASB). That gives support to the idea that we can begin when children are young to help them connect with God so that they can grow into a more intimate relationship with God in later years. Lest one believe spiritual growth in children is reserved only in the case of the Son of God, Scripture also suggests a similar process in the young lives of John the Baptist in the New Testament (Luke 1:80) and Samuel in the Old Testament (1 Samuel 2:26).

It is also interesting to note that at the time Jesus entered the temple at twelve years old, he was able to *amaze* the people listening to him with "His understanding and His answers" (Luke 2:47, NASB). In the twelve short years of his life, Jesus was able to experience and understand God in such a way that adult hearers were amazed. This is significant for our consideration today, because we realize that Jesus was also going through the common developmental aspects that all children go through. During his time of child development, Jesus was able to connect with God. In striving to be like Jesus, we can encourage children to strive to connect with God as well.

Using Developmental Science to Get an Understanding of Spiritual Possibilities

Understanding what children are thinking, what their intentions are, or what their motivations entail is often a difficult task for both a casual and scientific observer. To a greater degree, it is difficult to evaluate what is occurring spiritually in another person. For that reason, ministry leaders often turn to developmental science to fathom what potentials exist in the spiritual development of a person.

In the classic book, *Stages of Faith*, James Fowler (1981) explains how he created the faith development theory through combining the thoughts of Piaget's (1970) cognitive development theory, Kohlberg's (1976) moral development theory, and Erickson's (1963) psychosocial approach to human development.[63] While some researchers believe it is the interconnection of these various areas of human development that coalesce to create the spiritual development area, others believe the domain of spiritual development to be its own independent aspect.

Regardless of which side a person may hold to, it is fairly evident to most that spiritual development does interact with the other areas of development.[64] While other theories of development have been introduced to explain human growth and the seminal theories of Piaget, Kohlberg, and Erikson have been refined, the basic truth remains the same. The more proficient one becomes in understanding a child from the developmental sciences, the better one will be able to extrapolate what that same child may understand about the spiritual reality of God.

It is impossible to present much depth over childhood development in just a few paragraphs, and so it is recommended that leaders of children's ministry study the field. While some may object to studying developmental science because of its apparent lack of focus on spirituality, I believe science is really humanity's search to understand what God actually created. Although secular scientists may not recognize the Creator's role, that does not change the fact that God, in fact, is the Creator of people and the Organizer of how we develop. What follows will be a brief look at some major themes of development in the childhood years and an offering of suggestions that help parents and leaders contribute to the healthy spiritual growth of children. There is so much more to learn, but perhaps this will serve to whet your appetite for deeper study.

Developmental Milestones in Middle Childhood

Most children's ministries organize their ministry to include the age range of six-to-twelve-year-olds, or in practice, the ministry is usually based on the school system's divisions, including the range from first to fifth or sixth grade. How churches plan for sixth graders is another topic to be written about all in itself with unique considerations, but for our purposes we will include the sixth-grade child in our discussion.

Developmental scientists typically refer to this stage as *middle childhood*. Transition seems to be the key experience to describe the middle childhood phase, which begins with the significant transition of children beginning school and ends with the transition children experience at the onset of puberty.

One reason many cultures tend to start formal schooling for children around the age of six is because of the cognitive development that is occurring at this time. It is around age six or seven when children begin to have the ability to reason in order to make sense of the world around them. Piaget describes this stage as *concrete operational.*[65] Basically, in moving from the stages Piaget describes as *sensorimotor* and *preoperational* to the stage described as *concrete operational*, children are making the transition from action to thought. Children become able to solve problems by thinking about them.

This new cognitive ability is why some of the bedtime theology discussions with a child this age begin to occur. While more abstract and hypothetical thought abilities will not begin to be capable until in the late childhood or adolescent stage when *formal operational* thinking begins to develop, suffice it to say, it is during this stage that it becomes apparent that children are able to think about the concrete truths of Scripture and proclamations of God.

Not only are they able to contemplate the truths they hear about God, but also they are able to pray and communicate with God, who is already all about the business of communicating with them (and has been since before they were born).

The marker for the beginning of this stage also has a strong sociocultural tie, as it is associated with a child's greater association with the community outside of his or her parent's direct supervision. Children begin to spend many hours with teachers in schools, with coaches of various sports programs, with music teachers, with directors of dance and acrobatics, with ministry leaders at church, and in a variety of other activities. During these activities, children are also spending time with their peers while outside the control of parents. Although the parent's role remains central, the expanding social world of a child is becoming a greater influence in the shaping of a child's worldview. Erikson described the social aspect of this stage as one of *industry versus inferiority.*[66] He emphasized the role success in the new social platforms can play in contributing to a child's sense of competence and the role failure can play in a feeling of inferiority.

As a result of the increasing influence from those outside the walls of family, it is important to realize that children are beginning the process of making faith a part of their own realized experience. Although this is just the beginning, the ultimate goal is not for children to have a faith that merely imitates that of the parent but to have a faith that is true and personally experienced, a faith that is based on real encounters with God. Curriculum plans and Bible studies are effective when they share the revealed truths of God from Scripture to children in ways they can understand and begin to experience God in their lives. Our role is to be more than educators. We should strive to be leaders who impart opportunities for children to experience God personally.

As children move through middle childhood, they begin to develop a strong sense of self that is largely based on how they compare themselves with others. In the preschool and early part of this stage, children express themselves through ideas of fantasy. They take on the role of a mommy or daddy in their play, or perhaps a superhero or Star Wars character. (In working with preschoolers in ministry, I love to help children act out various Bible stories. They love being Daniel just as much as they love being the lions!) As children have greater exposure to outside learning environments and experiences that they begin to classify as successes or failures, they begin to assess themselves in comparison to others. Instead of having made-up super powers, they begin to accurately determine their abilities in academics, sports, and other activities. This leads children to create a sense of self. Also, they have moved further away from an egocentric view of the world and begin to understand things from the perspective of others. A simple illustration of being able to take the perspective of others is seen in how a preschooler is able to pinpoint his or her own left hand, but a child in the earliest part of middle childhood is now able to determine which is the left hand of another person. This capacity extends beyond the mere physical expressions to emotional expressions. They begin to consider how other people view them. They wonder whether they will be accepted. They start to feel pride when they accomplish a task well and embarrassment when they fail.

In developing a sense of self, a preschooler may go from pretending to have "bat vision" that lets them see things that are miles away to a child who believes he or she is horrible at soccer or art or some other activity. However, one positive thought to this accurate development of self that makes it entirely worth the journey is that children become more able to understand sin in their lives. While first it may come in comparing themselves with others, eventually they begin to understand sin in comparison to God. And, in understanding sin, they begin to understand their need for a Savior. Gaining an understanding of the need for the gospel definitely trumps the loss of fantasy super powers any day and is reason to rejoice.

The transition marker for the end of middle childhood is the onset of puberty. Just as children have finally grown into their reality and the way their body functions, things start to shake up as another transition begins to occur. Puberty begins at different ages for different children. For boys, puberty typically begins between twelve and sixteen, and for girls, it typically begins between ten and fourteen. When exactly this transition occurs in relation to one's peers often impacts some aspects of adolescent development and is a theme for another book.

Ministry Practices as Children Grow

So what does all of this mean in terms of practical application? Well, the development of children in this phase brings about new opportunities for ministry activities with children. Because children are beginning to differentiate from their parents and are becoming more comfortable in settings where they are on their own, a church is able to provide great support to children in helping them encounter God in a personal relationship.

Remember that the time in the first few years of middle childhood (first and second grades) is characterized by tremendous transition. In many ways these two years will resemble aspects of a preschool ministry. While play is beginning to fade in favor of new cognitive abilities, it is important to realize that different children will make the adjustment at different ages. Also, since we typically organize children based on grade levels, there is actually a wide range of ages in each group as well. For these two years in particular, play is still a needed aspect of a child's experience. Many ministries abruptly drop play centers from Bible study experiences at the beginning of middle childhood, when in fact a more gradual transition would be more appropriate. Do not be afraid to bring play into the learning environment.

In the middle years of middle childhood (third and fourth grades), churches often begin to offer opportunities for children to experience retreats and camp settings. This is more possible than before because most children have become accustomed to spending time away from their home and parents. While many factors come into play when offering camp experiences to children this age in order to create a safe environment, this is an appropriate age to begin to offer those opportunities. The programming at the camp should be age appropriate and appeal to a broad spectrum of developmental abilities and learning styles. A trend in children's camps exists that makes them look more like camps traditionally offered to adolescents, but a wise leader will make sure that camps for middle childhood participants fits their interests and abilities.

The latter years of middle childhood (fifth and sixth grades) are often called the preteen years and in actuality should have specific programming that helps differentiate them from children and prepare them for adolescence. Great consideration should be given to creating separate events and ministries just for this age group or for sixth graders alone. Kids at this stage need a safe environment that allows them to develop positive friendships and relationships that help them learn to live out their faith in their peer group. A strong preteen ministry can help kids grow in their relationship with God and stay connected to their faith community.

While coed Bible study experiences are appropriate in these age groups, there is an opportunity as children reach the preteen years for gender-specific ministries to provide a role in one's ministry strategy. There are some stereotypical differences in learning styles and interests of boys versus girls, but those do not always hold 100 percent true to a gender. The better reason to have gender-based ministries is that as children become teenagers, they will face different struggles based on their gender. Building strong Christ-centered friendships with their gender peers at this stage can be very helpful in developing relationships of accountability that will last through the sometimes tumultuous teenage years.

Conclusion

So as you can see from that brief journey through childhood, children definitely have many capabilities. They are growing, learning, and developing in some intricate ways, and all the while, God is intersecting in their lives to bring them into a more complete understanding of and relationship with him. Also, as you begin to understand children more, you will know better how to support them in their spiritual growth. The responsibility may seem great, but take encouragement in the words of Ephesians 2:10. "For we are His workmanship, created in Christ Jesus for good works, which God prepared beforehand so that we would walk in them" (NASB). In this verse, Paul said that we are the workmanship or handiwork of God and that God has prepared the good works that we will walk in before we even get to them. Rest assured that even though you may not know it, God is working in and through you to shape and fashion the children who are in your care. As you submit to following God, God will guide you in this great task.

Review Questions

1. How has the ministry you currently lead been influenced by your philosophy of children? What capacities for spiritual experience do you believe children have?

2. Do you see your role in ministry to children as merely an educator, or do you see opportunities to help children have real experiences with God?

3. In thinking about the children with whom you currently work and how they are developing a sense of self, what

biblical truths do you think are necessary to help inform them of God's view of them?

4. What types of ministries would you like to offer to specific groups in middle childhood? (preteen-specific ministries, gender-specific ministries, etc.)

5. What aspect of childhood would you like to study further in order to sharpen your skills and ability to help children connect with God?

Bibliography

Erickson, E. H.. *Childhood and Society*. 2nd edition. New York: Norton, 1963.

Fowler, James W. *Stages of Faith: The Psychology of Human Development and the Quest for Meaning*. New York: HarperCollins, 1981.

Green, Joel B. *The Gospel of Luke*. Grand Rapids, MI: Wm. B. Eerdmans, 1997.

Kohlberg, L. "Moral Stages and Moralization." In T. Lickona, ed. *Moral Development and Behavior*. New York: Holt, Reinhart and Winston, 1976.

Piaget, J. "Piaget's Theory." In P. Mussen, ed. *Charmichel's Manual of Child Psychology*. 3rd edition. Volume 1. New York: John Wiley and Sons, 1970.

Roehlkepartain, E. C., P. E. King, L. Wagener, and P. L. Benson, eds. *The Handbook of Spiritual Development in Childhood and Adolescence.* Thousand Oaks, CA: Sage Publications, 2006.

For Further Reading

Aamodt, S., and S. Wang. *Welcome to Your Child's Brain.* New York, NY: Bloomsbury, 2001.

Centers for Disease Control and Prevention. http://www.cdc.gov/ncbddd/childdevelopment/. Accessed 8/2/2014.

HealthyChildren.org - From the American Academy of Pediatrics. (n.d.). http://www.healthychildren.org/. Accessed 7/28/2014.

Land, J., ed. *Wholly Kids: Guiding Kids to Life in Christ.* Nashville, TN: Lifeway Press, 2012.

Levels of Biblical Learning. Nashville, TN: LifeWay Press, 2013. View or download from http://s7d9.scene7.com/is/content/LifeWayChristianResources/Levels-Of-Biblical-Learning-All-2013pdf. Accessed 8/21/2014.

Nye, R. *Children's Spirituality: What It Is and Why It Matters.* London: Church House Publishing, 2009.

Santrock, J. W. *Child Development.* 14th edition. New York, NY: McGraw-Hill Humanities, 2013.

Essential #5

DEVELOP SKILLS FOR SECURING SUPPORT FROM THE PASTOR, STAFF, AND CONGREGATION

By Cory Hines, Ph.D.

As Wayne began to reflect on the knowledge gained at his three-day national ministry conference, he dreamed of a truly transformational ministry to school-age children, their families, and those who serve them. He dreamed of a church body who saw this age group as a gift from God, one that requires nurturing, caring, and shepherding. In addition, he felt a prompting from the Lord to take a new and dedicated approach to developing the foundation of faith in each child in his church ministry. A ministry that was committed to seeing this through must partner with the parents and those who lead them at the church, so the seeds of faith can fall on soil that is properly cultivated through the early years of the child's life.

This type of ministry would not just happen; rather, it would take a dream, effort, hope, and endurance to become a reality. One key component in making this dream a reality is securing the support from the pastor, staff, and congregation of the church. This chapter will look at how these three groups can play a critical role in the success of leading an effective children's ministry to the children, families, and volunteer teachers.

The church of the twenty-first century demands strong pastoral leadership skills.[67] The congregation of today has a sense of expectation that those in leadership provide effective leadership. Today, more than ever, effectiveness is expected on the part of the pastor.[68] This is encouraging news to the leader of the children's ministry of the church, as this gives children's leaders the freedom to lead. The apostle Paul clearly identified God as the One who causes growth in the church (1 Corinthians 3:7), but God also tasks people to lead God's church (Titus 1:7). One of the primary responsibilities of a pastor is to lead.[69] It is important for the children's ministry leader to know and understand this, for the pastor is the one whom the Lord has tasked with providing leadership to the entire church body. Due to this, the effective children's ministry leader will work diligently to enlist the support of the pastor.

How to Secure the Support of the Pastor

There are a number of practical yet simple steps children's ministry leaders can take to help secure the support of their pastor. First and foremost, communication with the pastor is critical. No one likes to be surprised, especially your pastor. While your pastor does not need to know every little detail about the recently organized supply closet in your children's space, the pastor does need to be made aware when big things are taking place in your ministry. If a parent is being consistently negative about the children's ministry of the church, or if a children's volunteer has recently stopped serving, then you need to share this information with your pastor. It is important to keep the pastor informed and knowledgeable about the various things going on in the children's ministry. The pastor needs to be made aware of growth, struggles, success stories, and prayer needs, so proper pastoral leadership can be provided as needed.

Depending on how your church is structured, there are numerous ways in which you can communicate with your pastor. This might be a routine memo, an FYI e-mail, or even a weekly meeting. If at all possible, having a weekly meeting time with your pastor would be beneficial. If so, come prepared, and do not take too much time. One thing to consider might be coming to the meeting with the following discussion points: (1) things God did recently; (2) projects currently underway; (3) prayer needs; and (4) you need to know.

The *things God did recently* might include a report on a volunteer who had a breakthrough in some area of your ministry. It also might include a parent who has decided to start praying each night with his or her child. In discussing *projects currently underway*, do not get bogged down in the details. Rather, keep your pastor informed on the things you are working toward. This might be a remodeling project, curriculum studies you are conducting, or something similar. When sharing *prayer needs*, include key volunteer needs that have been expressed to you, as well as other needs that seem pressing. The *you need to know* portion is simply a time to cover any miscellaneous topics that you deem necessary to share with your pastor. Communicating with your pastor will go a long way in helping to secure your pastor's support for the children's ministry of your church.

Another way to help secure support is to show your pastor the role the children's ministry of the church is playing in helping to minister to the families in the church. Your pastor knows that your church wants strong, visionary, godly leadership.[70] Because of this, your pastor will be encouraged to hear how the children's ministry is ministering to the families in the church. As the leader of the children's ministry in the church, you need to champion and share how families are different because of the children's ministry. If there have been stories, letters, cards, e-mails, and so forth from people in your ministry that highlight the work the children's ministry is doing or has done in the past, then share that with your pastor. Let your pastor see how the children's ministry is influencing and making a difference in families. One tangible way your pastor can understand how the children's ministry of the church is impacting families is if your pastor has a child or children. If you are serving with a pastor who has a child in the children's ministry, make it a priority to minister to the child of your pastor just as you would any other family in your church. This will give your pastor a wonderful report on how the children's ministry is working to meet the needs of the families of the church.

One final way to secure support from your pastor is to give your pastor support. It has been said that serving as pastor of the average church might be the greatest and most complete leadership challenge imaginable.[71] Jesus said in Luke 6:31, "Do to others as you would have them do to you" (NRSV). Jesus commands us to put into practice with others what we hope and wish for them to put into practice with us. A children's ministry leader needs to give support publicly to his or her pastor. In training times, teaching opportunities, and in front of a group, it is important to show support of the pastor. In addition, a children's ministry leader who supports his or her pastor is one who routinely prays for the pastor. Something transformational takes place in the heart of a person who is praying for another person. God will soften your heart toward your pastor, fan the flames of trust with your pastor, and encourage you to follow the direction your pastor feels led by the Lord to lead the church. Supporting your pastor is biblical and will go a long way in gaining the pastor's much-needed support for effective leadership in the children's ministry of the church.

A children's ministry leader can do a variety of things to garner the support of the pastor, but these three will go a long way in getting the pastor's buy-in with respect to the children's ministry of the church. Communicating with your pastor helps your pastor see your passion and hear what is going on with your ministry. When you show your pastor how the children's ministry of the church is impacting families in the church, the children's ministry gains value and importance to your pastor and will help in gaining your pastor's support. By showing support to your pastor, you in turn will gain your pastor's support. Your pastor will be encouraged that you are making an effort to give support to the role your pastor is serving and will more than likely extend that same grace toward you. Once you have the support of your pastor, the task of gaining support from others will be significantly easier.[72]

How to Secure the Support of Other Staff Members

While enlisting the support of your pastor is important, it is vital to get the other staff members of your church to also be supportive of what the Lord is doing through the children's ministry of the church. As the leader, you need to strive to get your colaborers to embrace your vision with the same zeal and passion you possess.[73] When those who serve alongside you have an understanding of how the children's ministry of the church is impacting families, then they too will be supportive of the ministry you have been charged to lead. The wise children's ministry leader labors strategically to gain the support of the other staff members of the church.

One of the most valued parts of any ministry team in the local church is the volunteer. In order to garner the support of the other members of the church staff, the children's minister needs to cooperate with the other staff members of the church when recruiting volunteers. It is important that staff members see themselves as a part of a team.[74] Because so much of the ministry in a local church is done by volunteers, each church staff member is looking for called, capable, and willing volunteers. If the children's minister seeks to gain support from other staff members, then he or she would be wise to cooperate with the other members of the staff team. This can happen in a number of ways.

The children's minister who wishes to cooperate with other staff members in recruiting volunteers stays in contact with the other members of the church staff team. This may be a conversation between the two staff members or an update during a staff meeting, but whenever is appropriate for each situation, open communication with staff should be expected. Imagine that you, as the children's ministry leader, have identified a potential volunteer for your ministry. You see that the potential volunteer is invested in the ministry, is extremely active in your church, and has the personality makeup of someone whom you feel would make a great teammate. Considering that you are always on the lookout for good volunteers, you approach the potential volunteer after Sunday morning Bible study and ask whether he or she would like to meet with you this week about possibly serving in the children's ministry of the church. The key layperson smiles and then replies that he or she has been talking with the student minister of the church about leading a small group on Sunday or Wednesday nights. Needless to say, you are disappointed and feel somewhat in the dark that your student minister colleague did not alert you that he or she was recruiting new volunteers. Do your part in helping others on your staff team not feel this way by communicating openly and effectively with each of them.

Another great way to enlist the support of your staff team is to work together in training opportunities. Each member of the church staff knows that training must not be neglected, because if training does not take place, then people will be doing their own thing.[75] In order for each ministry of the church to be charging forward in the same direction, every staff member must be proactive in training his or her volunteers. As the children's ministry leader, there might be some things you could do with the other ministries of the church that would strengthen the training your volunteers receive, increase participation in training times, and add some variety in the training offered. One way to execute this for all of the different age-group ministries of the church is to have a combined training time, with breakout sessions that are led by each specific age-group leader. Consider bringing in a speaker such as a university professor or a published author to make a presentation to all of the volunteers in the ministry to children from birth through college. If your training budget does not have the necessary funds for this, consider whether one of the staff leaders of another age-group ministry is gifted enough to speak to the entire group of ministry volunteers. By suggesting and asking another age-group ministry leader of your church to speak to all of the volunteers, not only do you save your church some money, but you also will have gained more support from your ministry colleague. If the church budget allows, a nice meal can be served before the keynote talk, followed with breakout sessions focusing on specific ministry issues. By working together with others on your church staff team, you will gain their support for what God is leading you to do in providing direction to and shepherding the children and their families of your church.

Some expenses in ministry can be shared among the age-group ministries of the church. For instance, all educational ministries of the church have a need for supplies. Although diapers for pre-schoolers cost more than pencils for the student ministry, both are important for the ministries to succeed and excel. The children's leader who strives to develop support among his or her ministry peers will diligently search for expenses that can be shared. If there is a need for media purchases such as a new sound board or television, see whether it is possible to share costs between multiple age-group ministries. This will not only help in developing strong relationships of support among the staff but also will bode well for budget conservation and maximizing budget expenditures. Be creative, and open a line of dialogue among your ministry partners so as to better understand how you might be able to partner with them in stretching their budget dollars.

How to Secure the Support of Church Members

It has been stated that the pastor and other ministry leaders of the church need to be supportive of the children's ministry of the church. It is important that they see the ministry that is done with children, their families, and volunteers as something that adds value to the overall ministry of the church. This chapter has discussed how the children's ministry leader might garner support from others on the church staff, but that is not enough. The effective children's minister also realizes that the members of the church need to see the children's ministry as something of value and something that needs to be a major ministry emphasis within the church.

One way to enlist the support of the church body for the children's ministry is to be visible to the church body. Many times, the children's ministry is not visible to the overall congregation, as children primarily are housed in a location somewhat detached from the main sanctuary. In addition, most of the children's ministry activities of the church may take place in locations where adults do not congregate. Because of this, the children's ministry leader of the church needs to work with the pastor to find ways to be in front of the congregation, enabling the children's ministry leader's voice to be heard.[76]

One natural and somewhat easy way to accomplish this is through Vacation Bible School parents' night or by presenting Bibles to school-age children as part of a worship service. This demonstrates the commitment of the church to serve as a partner in the spiritual development of the child.[77]

Another great way to gain support from the church members for the children's ministry of the church is to be creative in how such recognitions are celebrated. As the leader of the children's ministry of the church, consider enlisting a team of volunteers who can bring a fresh word of celebration from the church during the time of recognition. There may be people in your church who wish to volunteer and serve in the children's ministry but who are not gifted teachers, and serving on this volunteer team would give them an opportunity to be involved. The children's ministry might also develop a brochure about the full ministry to children and distribute it during the service.

Many families welcome children into their homes through adoption or foster care, and so be proactive in deciding how your church celebrates these events as well. Decide what would be an appropriate way to recognize the family and the adopted child.

Another way that the children's ministry of the church might enlist support among the church members is by serving outside the church in a local ministry that ministers to mothers in the community. Regardless of the size of your community or church body, there is a need to bring hope to new mothers who find themselves with few options. Some new mothers do not have the support from their family that they need to be a successful parent. Many of these new mothers find themselves in dire need of basic necessities in caring for a child. The members of your church can be that support to a new mother who feels hopeless. If an existing ministry is already doing this, then consider partnering with them.[78] If there is not an existing ministry in your community, prayerfully consider whether the Lord is leading your church to establish a ministry to new mothers who may wish for some assistance.

Another great way to enlist the support of your church for the children's ministry is to sponsor a volunteer appreciation banquet. An event like this will go a long way in increasing support for the children's ministry of your church. Each volunteer in the children's ministry, along with his or her spouse, should be invited to this banquet. In brainstorming how to best to accomplish this, it is important to remember that in order to make a volunteer feel valued and appreciated, the recognition needs to be personal.[79] Such recognition does not necessarily need to be done one-on-one, but there does need to be an opportunity to acknowledge the service of everyone individually. This can be done by asking each person to come forward and receive a certificate of appreciation, or by showing a multimedia presentation of each volunteer serving. Regardless of how this is done, it is important to make the appreciation personal. If the children's ministry has a volunteer who has continually surpassed expectations, consider naming an award after this person. At each annual volunteer appreciation banquet, an award can be given to one volunteer who embodies the spirit of the one whose namesake is on the award. Regardless of how it is done, the effective children's minister takes as many opportunities as possible to make sure volunteers know how much they are appreciated.[80]

In Summary

Effective children's ministry makes a difference in the lives of families, the church, and the community. The children's ministry leader who seeks to be used by the Lord to influence families understands the need to enlist the support of the pastor, staff members, and the church. While there are a number of ways to accomplish this, this chapter has provided a few opportunities and ideas on how one might gain the support of the pastor, the staff, and the church.

Review Questions

1. What is one takeaway from this chapter that you could implement this week?

2. In thinking about which area needs the most attention, do you plan to work on enlisting the support of your pastor, fellow ministry leaders, or church members first? Why so? What is your strategy to accomplish this?

3. Who on your ministry team can serve as a source of encouragement and accountability to follow through on the action steps you plan on taking after reading this chapter?

Bibliography

Barna, George, ed. *Leaders on Leadership: Wisdom, Advice and Encouragement on the Art of Leading God's People*. Ventura, CA: Regal Books, 1997.

Barna, George. *The State of the Church*. Ventura, CA: Isachar Resources, 2002.

Bass, B., ed. *Leadership in Congregations*. Herndon, VA: The Alban Institute, 2007.

Couch, R. *The Ministry of Childhood Education*. 3rd edition. Nashville, TN: LifeWay Christian Resources, 2000.

Garland, Diana. *Family Ministry: A Comprehensive Guide*. Downers Grove, IL: InterVarsity Press, 2012.

Johnson, E., and B. Bower. *Building a Great Children's Ministry*. Nashville, TN: Abingdon Press, 1992.

Mims, Gene. *The Kingdom Focused Church*. Nashville, TN: Broadman & Holman Publishers, 2003.

Pope, R. *The Prevailing Church*. Chicago: Moody Press, 2002.

Rainer, Thom. *Surprising Insights from the Unchurched*. Grand Rapids, MI: Zondervan, 2001.

Selzer, E. "Effectiveness of a Seminary's Training and Mentoring Program and Subsequent Job Satisfaction of Its Graduates." *Journal of Research on Christian Education*, no. 17 (2008):25–53.

Essential #6

ENSURE QUALITY TEACHING FOR CHILDREN

By Charles Smith, M.A. Religious Education (candidate for Ed.D.)

Christopher and his family recently moved to town. Today is the first Sunday he and his family are visiting your church. He misses his friends at the church he previously attended. Christopher is nervous and not sure what to expect when he comes to your first-grade class.

Sarah is energetic and makes friends easily. She is usually the first child to arrive each week because her parents come early to serve as greeters in their adult Sunday School class. Sarah enjoys coming to your fourth-grade class and rarely misses a Sunday. Today she plans to complete the Bible learning activity she began last week.

Andrew enjoys sports and plays on a select sixth-grade soccer team. Many of the games are played on Sunday, and Andrew's family often misses church during soccer season. His parents believe playing soccer now will increase Andrew's chances of making the varsity team in high school.

Christopher, Sarah, and Andrew represent the many boys and girls in our churches today. Do you know a Christopher, Sarah, or Andrew? They may be in the Sunday School class you teach. How do you meet the needs of all the boys and girls in your class while ensuring quality teaching takes place?

Psalm 139 reminds us that God created each person as a unique individual: "For you created my inmost being; you knit me together in my mother's womb. I praise you because I am fearfully and wonderfully made; your works are wonderful. I know that full well" (Psalm 139:13–14, NIV). Knowing how God has "fearfully and wonderfully" created each child helps teachers ensure quality teaching occurs with boys and girls. Understanding how children grow and learn is important in knowing how to address their learning needs.

Know the Child

Scripture provides little detail about Jesus' childhood years. The Gospel of Luke offers this summary: "And Jesus grew in wisdom and stature, and in favor with God and man" (Luke 2:52, NIV). Luke identified four aspects of Jesus' growth—mental, physical, social, and spiritual—that characterize human development. These characteristics help us understand how boys and girls pass through logical stages as they grow, develop, and mature during the ages of six through eleven.[81] In *The Teaching Ministry of the Church*, Norma Hedin discusses the mental, physical, social, and spiritual developmental characteristics of children.[82] She identifies the following implications for teaching:

- Recognize the unique developmental needs of the age group you teach. Familiarize teachers with these unique needs and help them to see the implications and application.

- Choose curriculum materials that are appropriate for the age group.
- Be sensitive to the child's inabilities as well as his abilities. Do not ask him to do something he cannot yet do. For example, do not ask a first-grade student to read instructions to himself and do an activity. First graders vary in their reading abilities.
- Use the growing skills of classification, chronology, and memorization to involve children in meaningful learning based on biblical content. Bible skills such as memorizing verses, classifying books of the Bible, and preparing time lines for biblical events are excellent during the childhood years.[83]

Children at various ages share two common characteristics:

1. They are *concrete thinkers*. Children think literally and have difficulty understanding abstract terms. Avoid describing Jesus as, for example, *the bread of life* or using confusing terms such as *give Jesus your heart*. Do not use object lessons with young children.

2. They have *short attention spans*. How long is a child's attention span? Usually no more than one minute per year of life.[84] A nine-year-old cannot concentrate on one activity for more than nine minutes before needing a change.

Everyone has a preferred learning style that influences the way we receive and process information. This occurs in one of three ways—by seeing (visual), by hearing (auditory), or through movement (kinesthetic). Children learn continuously, and while they learn in a variety of ways, most boys and girls have a preferred learning style that involves seeing, hearing, or doing. Knowing a child's learning style can benefit teachers in planning activities that will stimulate and enhance his or her learning experiences.

Visual learners like to see things as they learn. These children tend to remember faces instead of names, are good readers, and have good imaginations. They respond best to teaching that includes painting murals; looking at pictures, maps, charts and illustrations; designing charts, graphs, and posters; writing letters, poems, and scripts; and working puzzles and mazes.

Auditory learners like to listen as they learn. These children best remember what they hear. They respond well to verbal instructions, and they may like to talk while engaged in activities. They respond best to teaching that includes singing and listening to music; hearing and retelling Bible stories; playing word games; listening to instructions; and discussing case studies.

Kinesthetic learners learn best when their bodies are in motion. These children remember best when learning is associated with physical activity. They respond best to teaching that includes movement: pantomime, drama, and reenacting Bible stories; playing games; playing musical instruments; and associating gestures or movements with words or expressions.

Children learn through their senses. The more senses involved in learning, the more children will remember.

Children learn by being actively involved in the learning process. Making choices gives children ownership in and responsibility for their learning.

All children learn by experiencing and doing. Playing, discovering, manipulating, and interacting are ways children experience the world around them.

Children learn from the examples of others. How do children learn to pray? By listening to adults pray. How do children learn to worship? By worshiping with adults.

Children also learn by repetition. The more times a child hears a Bible story, the more likely the child is to remember the details.

Organize for Teaching

Churches can ensure that quality teaching takes place by determining the best organizational structure for optimal learning. A church should look at the number of children enrolled and decide how groupings will occur. Whether a church has ten or one hundred children enrolled in Sunday School, the key to providing good learning experiences is organization.

There are different options to consider when deciding how children will be grouped together in Sunday School. Most churches typically group children ages six through eleven by their school grades. The basic reason for grouping children by grade or age is that "children of the same grade or age are more likely to have similar interests, needs, and abilities than are children of different grades or ages."[85]

Children's groups are usually referred to as a class or department. The recommended teacher-learner ratio for a children's department is 1:6. The recommended maximum enrollment of boys and girls per department is thirty. Every class or department needs a minimum of two unrelated adult leaders present at all times because of safety and legal issues. The basic leadership structure includes a department director and one or more additional leaders.

The chart "Grade and Age Combinations" illustrates possible combinations for grouping children for Bible study.[86] It is possible to have from one to any number of children's departments. If there is only one department, it will enroll children all across the age span. A church with enough children for two departments will most likely find the logical division is a department for first, second, and third graders (six- through eight-year-olds) and a department for fourth, fifth, and sixth graders (nine- through eleven-year-olds).

Grade and Age Combinations								
One Department		Two Departments		Three Departments		Six Departments		
Grade	Age	Grade	Age	Grade	Age	Grade	Age	
1	6	1	6	1	6	1	6	or multiple
2	7	2	7	2	7	2	7	depart-
3	8	3	8	3	8	3	8	ments for
4	9	4	9	4	9	4	9	each age
5	10	5	10	5	10	5	10	group
6	11	6	11	6	11	6	11	
All ages together		*Grades 1–3; 4–6*		*Grades 1–2; 3–4; 5–6*		*All grades separate*		

The creation of three departments is best when the groupings for first and second graders (six- and seven-year olds), third and fourth graders (eight- and nine-year-olds), and fifth and sixth graders (ten- and eleven-year-olds) are equally divided across the age span. A department for each grade and age group is necessary when the number of children in each department is about equal. Additional departments should be added as enrollments exceed the maximum in these departments.

An ideal teaching group size is one teacher for every four to six children, although a group can be one child and one teacher. Small teaching groups within a department are beneficial for several reasons.

1. *Small groups help build relationships.* Relationships are vitally important in teaching and ministering to children. Small groups help teachers get to know children better. Girls and boys can interact more easily with the teacher and with one another. Children can observe and model the attitudes and behavior of caring Christian adults.

2. *Small groups allow for individualized attention.* Teachers get to know children better within the small-group setting. Smaller groups are less intimidating and children can interact more freely with the teacher and one another.

3. *Small groups help teachers guide behavior and learning.* There is less opportunity for distractions and disciplinary problems in small groups. Teaching can become more intentional and focused as children engage in learning.

4. *Small groups encourage dialogue and questions.* Children are naturally inquisitive, and they learn by asking questions. *Why did God let that happen? How did Jesus do that?* As teachers answer questions, they help children understand the Bible and how it applies to their lives.

5. *Small groups encourage effective ministry.* Teachers can pray for and offer help to children and their families as they become aware of specific ministry needs.

The number of children in each grade differs from year to year. Before each Sunday School year begins, churches should review the organizational structure of the children's division to determine how many classes or departments are needed. Careful attention to organization helps ensure effective teaching and ministry take place.

Select Curriculum

Churches that desire quality teaching will provide curriculum that meets the spiritual and educational needs of boys and girls. Today there are many choices when considering curriculum for children, and churches are exploring multiple options.

Three important factors should be considered when choosing children's curriculum: it should be "activity oriented, Bible based, and child centered."[87] Activity-oriented curriculum is structured around teaching through activities. Bible-based curriculum focuses on teaching Bible truths. Child-centered curriculum emphasizes learning styles and the developmental needs of boys and girls.

Publishers often provide print or downloadable copies of their materials for churches to preview when choosing curriculum. The following publishers offer online samples of their children's curriculum.

Publisher / Address	Phone	Website
BaptistWay Press Baptist General Convention of Texas 333 N Washington Ave Dallas, TX 75246-1798	214-858-5100 888-244-9400	http:// baptistwaypress. texasbaptists.org
David C. Cook 4050 Lee Vance View Colorado Springs, CO 80918	800-708-5550	http://www. davidccook.com
Gospel Light 1957 Eastman Ave Ventura, CA 93003-8085	800-446-7735	http://www. gospellight.com
Group 1515 Cascade Ave Loveland, CO 80538	800-447-1070	http://www.group. com
LifeWay Christian Resources One LifeWay Plaza Nashville, TN 37234	800-458-2772	http://www.lifeway. com

Standard
8805 Governor's Hill Dr.   800-543-1353   http://www.
Suite 400   standardpub.com
Cincinnati, OH 45249

An evaluation guide will prove helpful when selecting curriculum to use with boys and girls. Texas Baptists have developed a detailed resource for evaluating strengths and weaknesses of preschool and children's literature.[88] (The brochure "How to Evaluate Literature for Preschoolers and Children" was prepared by Dr. Diane Lane, Baptist General Convention of Texas. It is free and can be ordered by calling Dr. Lane's office at 214-828-5287 or e-mailing her at diane.lane@texasbaptists.org.) This tool provides a rationale for the importance of creating a spiritual foundation and identifies specific characteristics that should be present in the structure of the literature. Here is a quick checklist for evaluating literature:

Checklist of Preschool/Children Literature Characteristics[89]

Does the literature
☐ have a Bible-based foundation?
☐ have doctrinally sound information?
☐ have authentic learning activities?
☐ have educationally sound content and activities?
☐ have a variety of learning methods?
☐ guide conversation?
☐ encourage critical thinking?
☐ have the child at the center of learning?
☐ have age-appropriate content?
☐ have life application statements that connect with Bible passages?

Curriculum choices are important, and the church should choose curriculum with careful attention. Curriculum enhances the teaching and learning experience. Keep in mind, however, "that it is not good curriculum that makes the teaching good but good teaching that makes the curriculum good."[90]

Guide Learning

Teachers guide learning throughout the session. Whether teachers are directing a small-group activity or leading worship in a large group, everything that takes place during the session should be age appropriate, address the needs of children, and consider their learning styles.

As children arrive, they are greeted by the department director or another teacher in the department. From a chart listing the learning activities, boys and girls may choose what they wish to do. Each teacher will have selected an activity from the leader curriculum material to prepare and lead. All activities should support the unit of study and engage children with the Bible study material. The department director will direct children to the small-group activity of their choice.

Guide Learning in Small Groups

As mentioned earlier in this chapter, small groups help build relationships, allow for individualized attention, limit distractions and potential behavior problems, prompt discussion, and encourage effective ministry. Small groups offer the best teaching and learning experience for boys and girls during the Sunday session. Small groups may serve to introduce a new unit of study or continue learning throughout a unit of study.

The following activities from a unit on Bible writers outline the intended purpose, provide instructions for the teacher, and give directions for leading the activities. Such activities can be used throughout the unit or stored for use again later.

Bible Learning Activity for First and Second Graders

Make a Bible Scroll

Purpose: to help children learn the unit Bible verses

Resources: Bible, picture of a scroll

Supplies:

- Paper
- Pencils or thin markers
- Tape
- Glue

- Dowel rods or cardboard tubes from coat hangers
- Yarn or ribbon
- Sheet of newsprint or poster board

Prepare: As you prepare to guide the activity, read the unit Bible verses from several Bible translations and paraphrases. Think about the meaning of the verses and how to explain them in your own words.

Gather supplies and materials: Gather enough paper for each child to have five sheets each. Cardboard tubes from coat hangers make inexpensive but sturdy dowel rods and can be cut to size. Print the unit Bible verses on a sheet of newsprint or a piece of poster board so they can be easily read. For first graders, print each verse on a separate sheet of paper with words missing for them to fill in the blanks. They may choose to draw pictures to illustrate words since their writing skills are limited. Place bookmarks in a Bible to mark each verse.

Lead the activity: Greet children as they arrive. Show them the printed Bible verses. Ask a child to open the Bible to one of the bookmarks. Help children see where the verse is found. Read the verse aloud. Continue in this way with all of the verses. Talk about the verses and look at pictures of a scroll. Give a brief overview of the Bible story. Guide the children to select a Bible verse and print it on the paper. As children work, guide the conversation toward the verses and their meaning. Help children connect their papers to the dowel rods and roll into a scroll. Tie with yarn or ribbon. Talk about ways to share their work with others. Ask children to help put away supplies and prepare for worship.

Pray: Thank you, God, for giving us the Bible. Amen.

Bible Learning Activity for Third and Fourth Graders

Match Bible Facts

Purpose: learn facts about the Bible

Resources: Bible, four-by-six-inch index cards (two colors)

Prepare: Study the Bible material for the unit and the Bible verses. Think about the Bible and the people who wrote it. Prepare a matching game by printing words and numbers on one set of index cards and the corresponding answer on a different set. The sets should be different colors. Use the following tables as your guide. Scramble card sets and place face down on the table.

Clue	Answer
Word meaning Bible	Biblia
Number of books in the Bible	66
Number of books in the Old Testament	39
Number of books in the New Testament	27
Hymn book of the Bible	Psalms
Good News	Gospel
First book of the Bible	Genesis
Tells the history of the early church	Acts
Last book of the Bible	Revelation
Shepherd, king, Bible writer	David
Doctor, Bible writer	Luke
Contains the Ten Commandments	Exodus
Old Testament prophet and Bible writer	Jeremiah

Lead the Activity: Welcome children to the group. Begin by reviewing the unit of study for the month. Talk about how God used different people to write the Bible. Give a brief overview of the unit Bible stories. Review the session Bible verse. Help children understand that the Bible is true and never changes.

Draw attention to the sets of cards on the table. Explain how the game is played. Allow each child to have a turn attempting to make a match. Help children understand Bible facts as matches are made. Allow children to use their Bibles if needed. Show the list of books in the table of contents of a Bible. Encourage play as time allows.

Pray: Conclude with prayer thanking God for the Bible.

Bible Learning Activity for Fifth and Sixth Graders

Develop Bible Skills

Purpose: to learn the books and divisions of the Old Testament and the New Testament

Supplies: Bible, sixty-six three-by-five-inch index cards, brown paper lunch sacks

Prepare: Print the names of the books of the Bible on separate cards. Print the following on separate lunch sacks: *Law, History, Poetry and Wisdom, Major Prophets, Minor Prophets, Gospels, History, Paul's Letters, General Letters, Prophecy*

Lead the Activity: Group lunch sacks according to the divisions of the Old Testament and the New Testament and stand upright on the table or floor. Remind boys and girls how God used different people to write the Bible. Explain that this month they will be learning how God used David, Jeremiah, Matthew, Luke, and Paul to write God's words. Help boys and girls understand that the Bible is a collection of sixty-six different books.

Draw attention to the lunch sacks and explain the two divisions of the Bible are the Old Testament, which tells of events before the birth of Jesus, and the New Testament, which tells about things that happened after Jesus' birth. Show the books of the Bible cards. Shuffle the cards and place face down in a stack.

Instruct children to take turns drawing a card from the stack. Read the name of the Bible book and place it in the appropriate sack. Allow children to use their Bibles if needed. Give guidance and offer help as needed. Continue as time allows or until all cards have been drawn.

Pray: Thank God for the people who wrote the Bible. Thank God that the Bible is true and never changes.

Teaching Tip: This is a good activity for early arrivers or to help the children continue to enjoy learning after they complete their work. This activity will store compactly in a plastic zip bag and can be filed with teaching resources for future use.

Transition

The department director will indicate when it is time to begin preparing for the large group. Children should be encouraged to gather supplies and materials and clear the work area. Teachers can assist as needed.

Guide Worship in the Large Group

Children and teachers come together to form a large group. An optimal seating arrangement is a semicircle with all people seated, including the director and teachers. The large group provides a worship experience for children at their level of understanding. Although it may differ in content, the outline for the large group should contain the following elements for all age groups:

Songs. Unit songs reinforce the Bible truths being taught. Choose a familiar hymn or chorus to sing during the month. Younger children may enjoy playing musical instruments as they sing. Third and fourth graders may choose a Bible verse they are learning and sing it to a familiar tune. Older boys and girls may write a poem and set it to music. Children express worship through each of these activities.

Bible story. Children learn Bible facts and discover Bible truths as they hear a Bible story. Teachers should always use an open Bible when telling the story. As they study about Bible writers, first and second graders learn that David was a shepherd who wrote songs. Third and fourth graders learn that Matthew and Luke wrote books in the New Testament. Fifth and sixth graders discover that the Bible books were not written in the order they are listed.

Bible verse. The Bible relates to the Bible story and the unit of study. It may be a brief Bible thought for younger children or a longer verse for middle and older boys and girls. Using the Bible verse during learning activities and throughout the teaching session is helpful when encouraging Scripture memory. Ask first and second graders to say the verse in unison. Encourage third and fourth graders to locate the verse in their Bibles. Challenge fifth and sixth graders to repeat the verse without looking at the words.

Review Bible story. A brief review helps determine how well children understood the Bible story. Use teaching pictures, questions, games or resource materials provided with your curriculum to review the Bible story. Younger children can identify key people in a teaching picture. Third and fourth graders can match clues with facts about the Bible. Older boys and girls can use role play to retell the Bible story.

Develop Bible skills. Children learn the Bible is God's word and that it is true and trustworthy as they develop Bible skills. First and second graders learn the two divisions of the Bible are the Old Testament and New Testament. Third and fourth graders can find a book in the Bible by saying the books in order and looking for the book in their Bibles. Older children learn to locate a passage in the Bible using a concordance.

Apply Bible truth. Children demonstrate understanding as they apply Bible truths in their own lives. As children learn about showing God's love to others, first and second graders can make cards to send to a sick child in the hospital. Third and fourth graders can collect cans of food to take to a local shelter. Fifth and sixth graders can plan a ministry project for an ill church member.

Express Bible learning. Boys and girls should have opportunity to share the work they have completed in their small groups. This is especially important on the final Sunday of a unit. Children who have worked on an activity or project during the month need to share with others what they have learned.

Pray. Conclude the session in prayer. Provide different prayer experiences for the children. Younger children find it easy to pray by completing a simple sentence such as, "Thank you, God for ____." Middle children are encouraged to pray aloud as they hear teachers pray during Sunday School. Older children can make a prayer chart listing specific requests for and answers to prayer.

Children learn to worship God through singing, praying, and listening to Bible stories as they participate in the large group. During this time, the director ties together the learning in the small group with life applications of the Bible content.

Plan for Continued Learning

On the first Sunday of a unit, time should be allotted at the end of the session to plan small-group teaching for month-long projects or learning activities. Children should help in planning, assign individual responsibilities, and discuss how the project or activity will be shared with others in the class. Children will continue learning in these groups at the beginning of each session for the rest of the unit.

Dismiss

Security and safety of children must be a priority for churches today. Teachers should know who will be meeting children at the conclusion of the session. Children should be released only to a designated family member or other adult.

Conclusion

The task of ensuring quality teaching for children is important and should not be taken lightly. Churches that value quality teaching for boys and girls commit to providing the best educational experience possible. They provide an organizational structure where children share and learn in both small and large group settings. Boys and girls develop relationships with peers and adults as they engage in learning activities and share worship experiences together.

Review Questions

1. Children share developmental characteristics. Identify ways the children you teach are growing physically, mentally, emotionally, and spiritually. What learning experiences can you provide that address these characteristics?

2. Review your church's organizational structure for children's classes or departments. What factors determine how children are grouped for learning?

3. Consider the importance of teaching in small groups. What other benefits can you add to the list from this chapter?

4. What can a church do to intentionally integrate children into the church's corporate worship experience?

For Further Reading

Anthony, Michael. *Introducing Christian Education*. Grand Rapids, MI: Baker Academic, 2001.

Barna, George. *Transforming Children into Spiritual Champions*. Ventura, CA: Issachar Resources, 2003.

Cloyd, Betty. *Children and Prayer: A Shared Pilgrimage*. Nashville, TN: Upper Room Books, 1997.

Eldridge, Daryl, compiler. *The Teaching Ministry of the Church*. Nashville, TN: Broadman & Holman, 1995.

Fuller, Cheri. *When Children Pray*. Sisters, OR: Multnomah Publishers, 1998.

Spooner, Bernard M., gen. ed. *Christian Education Leadership*. Coppell, TX: Christian Leadership Publishing, 2012.

Stonehouse, Catherine. *Joining Children on the Spiritual Journey*. Grand Rapids, MI: BridgePoint Books, 1998.

Yount, William R., ed. *The Teaching Ministry of the Church*, 2nd Edition. Nashville, TN: B&H, 2008.

Suggested Resources

How to Evaluate Literature for Preschoolers and Children. Available from Bible Study/Discipleship Center, Baptist General Convention of Texas, Dallas.

Levels of Biblical Learning and *Levels of Bible Skills*. Free download-able resources from www.LifeWay.com. They can be found in the Kids Ministry section. See http://www.lifeway.com/n/Product-Family/Levels-of-Biblical-Learning. Accessed 10/13/14.

Essential #7

DEVELOP CREATIVE APPROACHES FOR REACHING AND ATTRACTING CHILDREN AND THEIR FAMILIES

By Shelly Melia, Ph.D.

Dallas, Texas, is home to a massive highway interchange that locals refer to as the *Dallas High Five*. It is known as the *High Five* because it includes five levels of roadways stacked on top of each other, connected by thirty-seven bridges. The complexity of this interchange sometimes makes it challenging for drivers to master. In order to enjoy the benefits of this intricate roadway, drivers must first be able to locate and use an on-ramp. On-ramps provide an entry point for drivers. Roadway engineers strategically design on-ramps with a single purpose in mind: movement. After all, isn't that the purpose of a road? Roads are designed to move people from one location to the next with efficiency, speed, and safety.

The purpose of this chapter is to help the reader create and develop ministries and events that can serve as on-ramps for children and their families with the same singular purpose in mind: movement. In this case, movement relates to the Great Commission to make disciples (Matthew 28:19–20). Discipleship is a journey that is characterized by movement. For example, Luke 2:52 indicates Jesus' childhood was full of movement and growth: "And Jesus grew in wisdom and stature, and in favor with God and man" (NIV). Unfortunately, churches can often look like the *Dallas High Five* during rush hour traffic and may overwhelm and intimidate families with multiple layers of programming and ministry.

Collaboration Is Essential

Civil engineers understand the importance of collaboration in the development of road design. Imagine the disaster that would occur if engineers operated independently and without input and assistance from community stakeholders and construction specialists. Likewise, churches must understand and be committed to increasing levels of collaboration as they seek to reach and integrate unengaged families into the discipleship process. The mission and vision of the church must be consistently communicated and fleshed out through intentional, purposeful ministries that create movement toward or within the discipleship journey. Collaboration relates to the necessity of a holistic approach in ministry to the entire family. In essence, collaboration is the way in which multiple ministries stack hands and seamlessly provide on-ramps leading to one destination: discipleship.

In order to understand the importance of collaboration, consider this example of a church that lacked collaboration in its efforts to reach children and their families:

> The Jones family recently moved to a new town and needed to find a program for their two children to attend after

school and during the summer. After polling their Facebook friends in the area and viewing numerous websites, they decided the Child Development Center at the First Baptist Church in their new hometown was the right fit. They weren't necessarily looking for a church-based program, but they liked what they saw when they took a tour. After all, they had grown up going to church on a fairly regular basis, and they considered themselves spiritual, just not religious.

When they first enrolled their child in the program, the church sent them a letter welcoming them to the church and thanking them for the opportunity to care for their children. Other than that, very little contact was made from anyone at the church. They attended their children's seasonal programs in the worship center, but they never set foot into the church other than for the services the church provided. Most of the teachers did not attend church there on Sunday, and so the Jones family never got a personal invitation to attend worship or get connected in a Bible study group.

The children of the Jones family were in after-school care five days a week until the time each child entered middle school. Once the Jones kids no longer attended the programs, the family's relationship with the church ended.

Unfortunately, this is an all-too-familiar story. The Joneses represent a snapshot of millennial parents (parents born between 1980 and 2000). Millennial parents often consider themselves spiritual, but they aren't necessarily interested in committing themselves to the institution of the church.[91] Focus on the Family puts it this way:

Many millennials without specific religious identification express beliefs and behaviors demonstrating some type of spiritual belief. Of course, this type of "generalized faith" is not something to celebrate, nor is it necessarily cause for despair. They are not—as some might suggest—becoming hardened atheists or agnostics. They are open to spiritual truths.[92]

Further, a recent Pew Research study found that one-third of adults under age thirty are religiously unaffiliated.[93] George Barna echoed this sentiment in finding that only 20 percent of millennials believe going to church is important.[94] Clearly, there are families who need to be reached, and many times they are within an arm's reach of the church. However, when there is no collaboration among ministries, families like the Joneses become merely consumers of services. If the goal was to fill up the rooms in the church five days a week, then the Jones family helped the church accomplish their goal. If the goal was to provide ministry that created on-ramps for children and their families to become engaged in discipleship, then the church might have created some congestion, but no movement.

Collaboration Creates Synergy

Merriam-Webster defines synergy as the "increased effectiveness that results when two or more people or businesses work together."[95] Synergy occurs in the local church when two or more ministries collaborate to meet the increasingly complex and diverse needs of young families. The minister to children will not have the same success in reaching a young family as the combined efforts of the pastor, minister to children, minister to adults, and volunteers. While attracting children and their families to church is important, developing a strategy to integrate the entire family into the discipleship process is the most essential task of the church in reaching families. To put it simply, churches do not have a problem attracting children and their families to the abundance of activities and ministries within the church; rather, churches have a problem assimilating families into the discipleship process.

Consider for a moment what might have been done differently to engage the Jones family by executing a strategy that included collaboration and synergy:

> The Jones family moved into a new community and quickly began searching for child care for their two children. Mom used social media to poll her friends in the area about which program was the best. Her friends suggested the after-school program at the First Baptist Church.

> A visit to the church's website provided detailed information about the program. The website had a tagline on it that resonated deeply with both parents: "We prepare children to make a difference in the world, one child at a time." The church webmaster had studied millennials and worked hard to design web pages that spoke their language.

> Mom and Dad scheduled an appointment to tour the center and were greeted warmly by the director. They were impressed with the facilities and with the teachers, who spoke highly of the church's desire to do more than just babysit children.

> A few days later, they brought their children to the center for their first day. They were elated when they picked up their children and the children had already made friends.

> A week later the Joneses received a handwritten note and package from the education minister. The education minister thanked them for the privilege of caring for their children and told them about a new Bible Study class for parents

their age that would start in just a few weeks. Included in the package was a DVD containing a message from the pastor about the important role of a parent in laying foundations of faith for their children.

The next day, when the Jones couple dropped their children off, the teacher handed them a flyer about a new sermon series beginning that Sunday on parenting. One teacher even invited them to come and sit with them. As weeks turned into months, the Joneses became more open to the church.

During the summer, the Jones children had an opportunity to interface with the church staff on a more regular basis. The minister to children and minister of music enlisted volunteers to do a music camp with the participants in the summer day camp. On one Sunday in July, the kids were invited to share their musical with the church during the regular worship hour. The staff and volunteers in the church took great care to make sure the families were warmly welcomed and treated as honored guests. For many of the parents, it was their first time to visit the church on a Sunday morning.

During the abbreviated sermon time, the pastor spoke passionately about the church's strategy to reach children and prepare them to make a difference in the world. After the service, families were served lunch by the volunteer members of the Bible study group in the church that fit their demographics. The Joneses were impressed when they met a young couple who seemed genuinely interested in their family. A personal invitation was extended to the mom to attend a women's Bible study on Wednesday night. Mr. Jones was surprised when he was asked to attend a men's ministry camping trip. As they were driving home, they decided to take the couple up on their invitation. After all, Mrs. Jones was looking to meet new friends, and Mr. Jones loved camping.

In the second version of the story of the Jones family, there was a high level of collaboration with at least three different prongs of influence. First, there was the ministry itself: the after-school and summer day camp program of the church. The minister to children, director of the program, and the teachers themselves understood their mission was bigger than just taking care of the children, and they each did their part in executing the overall strategy. The second prong was the church staff. The pastor and education minister, along with the minister to children, provided support and influence through the website, a personal letter, high-quality video, relevant sermon series, and their presence at big events. Finally, perhaps most importantly, the third prong consisted of church members who showed up to serve the families after the program. Few things speak louder to millennial parents than their peers inviting them into the community.

But We Don't Have the Time or the Resources for All That Collaboration!

Is it realistic for a church to be able to tackle every event or ministry with the level of collaboration and synergy found in the second story of the Joneses? It's a legitimate question. However, maybe a better question would be this: If we aren't able to effectively execute our strategy, then why are we continuing to do the event or ministry?

Churches with complex ministries and no clear discipleship process are in decline and are often too busy to notice the people around them who need to be reached.[96] On the other hand, churches that understand the most important aspect of reaching people is developing a simple discipleship strategy based on authentic relationships tend to thrive and expand the kingdom.[97]

Church Websites and Social Media—the Front Door to the Church Today

Churches who want to reach children and their families understand the importance of providing an up-to-date website and the necessity of an active presence on social media. Parents of children are often referred to as digital natives and are always connected by means of technology.[98] The term *digital native* refers to the fact that this generation of parents has grown up without having to adapt to technology. Technology is all they have ever known and their primary means of information acquisition.[99] Barna research notes this about young parents: "The first and last thing most people do every day is check their phones. When they want to know an answer to a question, they Google it. Scrolling through Facebook, Instagram, and Twitter feeds has become a fixture of leisure activity."[100]

In addition, church webmasters should make sure website content communicates the heart of the church. Millennial parents are drawn to causes they can become passionate about, and the website provides an opportunity to breathe life into the mission and vision of the church while being careful not to overemphasize the institutional nature of the church.[101] The church website is a crucial component in providing a digital road map, but it is not the final destination for most users. Church websites that also actively promote their social media outlets understand that parents begin at a website but prefer updates and connection through social media.[102] Finally, consider thinking *mobile first* in the design of the website. Roughly 80 percent of this generation have smartphones, and as many as 20 percent of them access the Internet exclusively through their smartphones.[103]

Creating Ministries and Events That Serve as On-Ramps for Children and Their Families

Now that we understand the importance of collaboration, synergy, and digital road maps, it is time to talk about the ministries and events themselves. Ecclesiastes 1:9 reminds us, "What has been will be again, what has been done will be done again; there is nothing new under the sun" (NIV). Certainly, there are very few new ideas when it comes to reaching people. However, some ideas have stood the test of time and have been fairly successful in reaching children and their families.

Vacation Bible School is one of the most common outreach events designed specifically for children. However, Jerry Wooley, LifeWay Christian Resources Vacation Bible School specialist, warns that attendance at VBS does not always equal effective outreach: "[F]or too long we have made VBS the event of the summer. Connecting with millions of people but making a lasting impact with only a small percentage."[104] Wooley suggests that a better measure of success for VBS than enrollment numbers would be the number of previously unchurched families who remain connected to the church a year later.[105] Here are some ideas about how to continue the connection after VBS:

1. Enlist a specialized team of volunteers who are laser focused on follow-up with unchurched families. This team should have no responsibilities in VBS other than follow-up.

2. Design the enrollment process so that unchurched families can be easily identified and contacted by telephone, mail, or e-mail. Online registration can help streamline this process as reports can be generated and used to empower volunteers as they strive to continue the connection established during VBS. At the end of the week, e-mail every department

director a list that contains the contact information of the children in their class who are unchurched.

3. Provide road signs during the week that point families to future involvement with the church. Promote the church website in all written communication and highlight upcoming opportunities for families to get involved. All church staff members should find creative ways to communicate with the captive audience of parents during the week of VBS. VBS is not just an event driven by the minister to children; it requires the support and participation of all staff members.

4. Family night at VBS can provide a great opportunity to expose unchurched families to authentic relationships in the context of the local church. Be strategic in enlisting volunteers from various Bible study groups in the church to serve and interact during family night. Create a culture of movement as you train volunteers to understand their role in helping families find appropriate on-ramps that lead to discipleship.

5. Start a new Bible study group at the completion of VBS for parents of children. Encourage the teachers in the new class to personally invite every unchurched family from VBS. In addition to personal contact, use e-mail or social media to get the word out about the new class. Consider sending home a flyer with a QR code that can be scanned using a smartphone. Once the code is scanned, the user could be sent a website that contains an online greeting from the pastor and new teachers. Finally, seed the class with a few trained and committed couples who will be outreach focused. This will help ensure the class gets off the ground and will help the energy and dynamics of the new group.

Another example of a ministry designed to serve as an on-ramp for children and their families is the recreation ministry. Some churches choose to offer Upward Sports as a means of engaging unreached children and their families.[106] The mission of Upward Sports is "Promoting the Discovery of Jesus Through Sports." Basketball, soccer, volleyball, baseball, cheerleading, and flag football leagues provide opportunities to teach children athletic skills with a heavy emphasis on evangelism and discipleship. Upward Sports meets a need for young families and often includes a high percentage of unchurched families. Consider these ideas for creating movement in the discipleship process through the ministry of recreation:

1. Enlist and equip coaches to serve as a bridge to the church. Train the coaches to work alongside the church in ministering to families on the team who may have experienced a new birth, a death, an illness, or any of a number of family crises. Encourage the coach to make personal invitations to events at the church as they become acquainted with the parents in the class.

2. As part of each game, Upward Sports encourages churches to enlist volunteers to share brief testimonies with the crowd. These can be salvation stories or testimonies of God's faithfulness. This can be an effective way for volunteers to interface with families who need to hear the good news of Jesus Christ.

3. Strategically plan end-of-season celebration events for the entire family. Churches may enlist a special speaker or plan a family night at the church with activities that children and their parents can enjoy together. Be sure to include staff and volunteers from the church who are trained to interact

and develop relationships with the families. Provide road signs in the form of flyers, PowerPoint slides, banners, website promotions, or e-mails that include a word about next steps in terms of ways to get involved in the church.

Collaboration with the women's ministry in the church can also provide a great on-ramp for children and their families. A weekday Bible study or prayer group for mothers of children could be established with the primary focus of outreach. George Barna found in his research that three-quarters of moms indicated their faith was an important part of their lives. Barna also found that the "spirituality of moms outpaces that of dads."[107] Moms tend to be more open to faith and spirituality, and moms of children typically need relationships with other moms. Some churches also match young mothers with veteran mothers to serve as mentors. These mentoring relationships provide an opportunity to "move on to maturity through friendship, wisdom, and support. Young adults are drawn to churches that believe in them enough to challenge them."[108]

Summer camps, retreats, and other one-time events provide additional opportunities to create on-ramps for children and their families. Children need opportunities to develop strong relationships with children and significant adults in the church. Spending several days away with the children's ministry often results in an opportunity for a child to make a decision to follow Christ. Counselors should be trained to share the gospel in age-appropriate ways, and special care should be taken in planning evangelistic appeals to children so that children aren't manipulated or encouraged to make premature decisions.

Another obvious connection for children and their families occurs at Christmas. Some churches have great success in producing a live nativity that provides an experiential learning approach to the story of Jesus' birth. Families enjoy attending creative events that depict the birth of Christ. Advertise in the local newspaper as well as on the website and through social media. Church members could put yard signs in their yard to draw attention to the big event. Collect information on each family in attendance, and enlist a team to follow up with each guest.

Conclusion

The focus of this chapter has not been on providing an extensive list of creative ministries and events that can be developed to attract children and their families to the local church. The ideas and possibilities are endless. As a matter of fact, a quick Internet search for "creative events to attract children and their families" netted more than 2,000,000 results in just .62 seconds.

The emphasis of the chapter has been on understanding how to create more than just fun, trendy, and often expensive one-time events, though. For too long, churches have measured success in terms of attendance numbers. The result has been very little long-term growth or movement in the discipleship process. Millennial parents are not interested in being busier. They are looking for authentic relationships and opportunities to make a difference in their world. In today's context of family, it will take high levels of collaboration and synergy in order to begin to see the kind of movement that results in effective discipleship.

Review Questions

1. Do you agree or disagree with this statement: "Churches do not have a problem attracting children and their families to the abundance of activities and ministries within the church;

rather, churches have a problem assimilating families into the discipleship process."

2. How can churches encourage collaboration and synergy when planning new ministries to attract children and their families?

3. What is meant by the need for a holistic approach to children and their families?

4. Does your church measure success by attendance or by movement and engagement? What could you do to help your church move toward measuring success based on movement and engagement?

For Further Reading

Beckwith, Ivy. *Postmodern Children's Ministry: Ministry to Children in the 21st Century*. Grand Rapids, MI: Zondervan, 2004.

Mancini, Will. *Church Unique: How Missional Leaders Cast Vision, Capture Culture, and Create Movement*. San Francisco, CA: Jossey-Bass, 2008.

Renfro, Paul, Brandon Shields, and Jay Strother. *Perspectives on Family Ministry*. Nashville, TN: B & H Publishing Group, 2009.

Essential #8

PROVIDE APPROPRIATE QUALITY MINISTRY TO CHILDREN AND THEIR FAMILIES

By Marcia McQuitty, Ph.D., with Shelly Melia, Ph.D.

One of the most inspiring stories in the Old Testament describes the desire of a parent who desperately wanted to conceive and bear a child. Hannah, the wife of Elkanah, believed in the power of God, the Creator of the earth (1 Samuel 1). As the years went by, Hannah became more distressed and called out to the Lord.

"Making a vow, she pleaded, 'Lord of Hosts, if you will take notice of Your servant's affliction, remember and not forget me, and give Your servant a son, I will give him to the Lord all the days of his life, and his hair will never be cut'" (1 Sam. 1:11, HCSB).[109]

After an undisclosed amount of time had passed, the Lord remembered Hannah and her prayer. She conceived, and when the baby boy was born, she named him Samuel, because she said,

"I requested him from the LORD" (1 Sam. 1:20). Hannah kept her promise to the Lord, and when the boy Samuel was weaned, she took him to the Lord's house and gave him to Eli. She explained to Eli that she had promised the Lord that if the Lord gave her a son, she would "give the boy to the LORD. For as long as he lives, he is given to the LORD" (1 Sam. 1:28). As Hannah took her precious Samuel to live in the place of worship with Eli, the priest, did she ever wonder about Samuel's safety and about his living in a clean environment with a man who would care for him as if Samuel were his own son?

In another period of time, there lived a child who was the son of a preacher. His name was Adoniram Judson. "In any generation, Adoniram would be hailed as a precocious child—reading the Bible at three, fascinated by the world of languages, mathematics, and precise logic. His minister father was as aware as any parent watching a firstborn and exerted every pressure toward excellence."[110] When Adoniram was a child, did he attend church meetings where he was placed in safe and appropriat learning environments?

Years have passed since Adoniram Judson and his friend Luther Rice traveled to Asia to take the message of Jesus to people living in spiritual darkness. Today we have parents who teach biblical truths to their children in the home, but parents also bring their children to church. There they are placed in appropriate learning environments and taught by trained teachers who instruct them in biblical knowledge. Are these church environments safe and secure?

> When parents bring their child to church, they are bringing their most prized possession.

When parents bring their child to church, they are bringing their most prized possession. After the Sunday School session, parents expect to pick up a happy and contented child, having been treated with the best possible love and care while being taught biblical truths in a way that the child can understand. This expectation is not unrealistic. The person in charge of the children's division will be the one responsible to pay close attention to the details that will provide quality ministry.

Safety and Security

For some families, church becomes almost like a second home. The children know and love their teachers and feel confident and at ease in navigating through the church buildings and hallways. In time, parents may become so familiar and comfortable with the ministries offered to their children that they become complacent in terms of safety and security. However, it takes only one lost child or a timely news story concerning child abuse to cause parents and churches to be on high alert. Unfortunately, reactionary safety and security is the least effective way to minimize risk and prevent crises before they happen. Consider this story:

> John and Lisa were the parents of three children. The oldest was thirteen, and they also had twin boys who were eight years old. It had become a matter of routine for their thirteen-year-old son to pick up the twins each Sunday after Sunday School. The parents were in a class that often did not finish on time. The fact that the thirteen-year-old picked up the twins seemed to help make sure they would not be the last ones to be picked up. When the parents initially approached the teacher about this arrangement, she was hesitant but agreed to give it a try in order to help them out (and she was also growing weary of staying after the class session, waiting for the parents to pick them up).
>
> The arrangement was working well until one Sunday there was a miscommunication between the parents. John and Lisa had taken separate cars to church in order for John to help serve the Lord's Supper at the early service. After

church, John thought Lisa was bringing the kids home, and so he quickly left. Lisa thought she remembered that John had said he would bring the kids home, and so she took the opportunity to stop by the grocery store on the way home to pick up lunch. Since the twins had been picked up, the children's minister thought all the kids were gone, and so she had left to go home as well. Meanwhile, the kids were in the gym playing. They hadn't noticed that no one else was in the building. It wasn't until Lisa got home that John realized the kids were still at church and that they were unsupervised. Panic set in, and they both jumped in the car and rushed to find the kids unharmed, playing in the gym.

In this case, the children were not hurt. However, to make matters worse, the church was located in the downtown, metropolitan area of a large city. It was not uncommon for people to wander in off the streets looking for food or financial help. What could have happened to these unsupervised children? More importantly, how had the church leadership failed to provide a secure environment? What needed to change in order to make sure the situation never happened again?

These instances occur far more frequently than churches care to admit. Sometimes parents laugh it off as their mistake. However, churches should never take lightly the safety and security of each child. Churches cannot become complacent and comfortable when it comes to developing and implementing policies aimed at protecting children and their families.

The church must become adept at risk management and prevention. When children are in the care of the church, the church becomes responsible and liable for those children during any and all activities and ministries sponsored by the church. This includes both on-campus and off-campus events (camps, retreats, field trips, etc.). The list of potential risks in accepting responsibility for the care of minors is endless. There are natural disasters for which to plan, abuses to prevent, injuries to avoid, proper teacher-to-student ratios to maintain, background checks to be conducted, and the list could go on and on and on. Unfortunately, churches also have to be prepared for lawsuits that may be brought against them in the event of a breach in safety or security.

Several key components should be considered when a church is developing and implementing policies and procedures to minimize the risks associated with ministering to children and families. For the purposes of this chapter, focus will be limited to just two crucial areas—drop-off and pickup procedures and leadership enlistment policies. Keep in mind, not only must churches have these procedures and policies in place—they *must* also follow them *consistently*.

> Parents who are members of the church should be given a list of the policies and procedures for the children's ministry before the child promotes into the children's division.

As children move out of the preschool ministry and into the children's ministry of the church, parents are less likely to walk their child to the child's room and may expect teachers to dismiss their child without the presence of a parent. In some ways, this is a normal developmental milestone in that children are becoming more independent and may feel increasingly comfortable and confident in their ability to find their classroom or their parent. While independence is desirable, the safety of all children is the number one priority. Parents must be encouraged to walk their child to the classroom and follow the drop-off and pickup procedures outlined by the church.

When a parent accompanies his or her child to the classroom door for drop-off, it does several things. First, it allows the teacher to get to know the parent and begin to develop a relationship with the entire family. Sadly, many parents don't know the names of their child's teachers because they never interface with the teachers.

Second, taking the child to the classroom supports the security system that is in place and assures the parent that teachers will not allow anyone to pick up his or her child who isn't authorized to do so. This is especially important if there are custody disputes or legal issues that create confusion or distress for the child. Finally, when a parent picks up his or her child, it gives teachers an opportunity to share what the child learned or communicate any victories or challenges the child may be having.

One of the ways churches are standardizing drop-off and pickup procedures is through the use of technology. Numerous electronic programs can be used to check in children when they arrive at the church. Typically, a parent checks the child in at a computer kiosk in the hallway. These kiosks can be self-service or full-service and are usually manned by a volunteer or children's ministry staff representative. A name tag is printed for the child, and a security tag is printed for the parent or guardian. The security tag and name tag contain a security code that must be matched in order for the child to be released. Special instructions or allergies can also be listed on the name tag so teachers are well informed of any special needs a child may have.

Leadership Enlistment Policies

Not only do churches need to be consistent in enforcing drop-off and pickup policies, but they also must have a strong policy in place for leadership enlistment. Churches in every community need to guard against the threat of pedophiles.

Pedophiles are constantly on the lookout for places where they may be able to gain access to children. The local church needs to make sure that such a person will not be

> The first step in providing an environment that will protect children from sexual predators is to make church members *aware* of the dangers.

114

allowed to teach or even assist a teaching staff in the classroom. This calls for having in place a careful screening system that all people must go through in order to be allowed to teach in a classroom with minors. The first step in providing an environment that will protect children from sexual predators is to make church members *aware* of the dangers.

Sexual predators have invaded churches where fewer protective measures are in place. The bare minimum prevention techniques require the following steps to be taken:

1. *Require criminal background checks of all volunteer and paid workers.* (Lawyers and others who are aware of the statistics involving potential child molesters know that only a small number of these people have actually been caught and convicted. Therefore, a criminal background check will catch only those who have been caught and convicted. Doing background checks will also expose offenses involving violence, dishonesty, illegal substances, indecency, and any conduct contrary to the mission of the church. The background check application form and the results will need to be kept on file by the church.)

2. *Use security cameras in hallways and classrooms.* (Security cameras do not stop molestation or other forms of abuse, but they will record the offensive behavior and the grooming process leading up to the actions.)

3. *Use check-in systems to ensure that only an authorized person can take the child to and from the classroom.* (Parents need to understand that they cannot allow one of their children to bring the child to the room. Taking children to and from their room is the parent's or designated adult's responsibility. This also helps the teacher develop a relationship with the parent.)

4. *Implement a six-month member rule before a person is allowed to work with children.* (People interested in molesting or abusing children are interested in the *now* opportunity, not having to wait six months. This simple rule may discourage the molester and cause him or her to seek another place of opportunity.)

5. *Have two unrelated adults in the room with the children at all times.*[111]

A church-wide sexual abuse training course should be made available as a way to make church members aware of the seriousness of the situation in our world today.

A church-wide sexual abuse training course should be made available as a way to make church members aware of the seriousness of the situation in our world today.

A minister of education shared the following story of encountering a possible sexual predator in the church parking lot during a fall festival outreach event:

Church members had been enlisted to provide activities and special child-centered experiences from the trunks of their cars, which were situated in a large circle on the church parking lot. One of the deacons noticed that a person unknown to him was in the circle and was giving out comic books to the children. The deacon immediately went and told the minister of education about the suspicious person and activity. The minister of education went to meet the person. When the minister of education began asking questions, the man quickly got into his car and drove away. One of the children gave the minister the comic book he had received. On the inside cover was an invitation to meet the unidentified man in the neighborhood park on a given Saturday. Was the suspicious man a sexual predator? No one knew for sure, but his activities could not be dismissed when they involved the potential for hurting children.

Having enough teachers is a must. When parents bring their children to church, they expect them to be cared for and taught biblical truths by well-trained teachers. For a top quality and safe environment for teaching, two adults (not married to each other) need to be in the room when the first child arrives. Sometimes churches will want to use older teenagers in the classrooms. If and when this occurs, two adults still need to be in the room at all times. To ensure that all children will have their individual needs met while at church, the following child/teacher ratio needs to be followed:

| First to sixth graders | one teacher for every six children |
| Room size | twenty square feet for every child |

Communicating with Parents or Grandparents

Not all children are blessed with Christian parents and grandparents. But all parents and grandparents who bring children to church expect them to be cared for well while they are being taught biblical truths.

Who are these parents and grandparents, and how can the church minister to them? Consider whether these generalizations apply to the young parents you know. They live in a world of technology and thrive on keeping connected through Facebook, texting, e-mails, and phone calls. They live in a world of instability, constant movement, change, and anxiety. Their mind-set provides them with a no-patience attitude while they thrive on instant gratification. They look for new ways of thinking and processing information rather than valuing tradition. They are more interested in accumulating experiences rather than stuff and have a craving for authenticity. The young adults in our world are defined by four markers:

- *Community.* They want to know people deeply and experience a real relationship that will allow them to get to know someone personally.
- *Depth.* For example, they want to know the depths of the Bible.
- *Responsibility.* They want to make a difference in the world.
- *Connection.* They want to connect with other generations and want intergenerational mentoring.

We are living in a day in which there exists a wide age range among adults who have children. People with the responsibility of ministering in the children division would benefit from having an understanding of how parents/grandparents of children think in order to reach them more effectively. Older parents may be involved in a career outside the home that gives them little time to be with their children. Older parents or grandparents may be more interested in keeping the methods and classroom experiences the way they were when they themselves were children. We first need to understand that the children's division exists for the purpose of teaching biblical truths to the child and then effectively communicate this to the parents of all ages.

Few parents of children have been trained in an understanding of child development and in the methodology of Christian education. They may not know how to teach biblical truths to each age group in a way that maximizes learning. The children's minister can help parents learn how to teach spiritual truths to their children.

Parents will have many ideas that they have gleaned from listening to their friends. They have access to the Internet and can explore various fun and entertaining curriculum materials in a matter of minutes. When they find something new and exciting to them, they will often bring the idea to the church in hopes that it can be implemented there. Parents want to help. But they themselves need help with the basics.

After teaching a Sunday School class, I was walking down the hall toward the sanctuary for the morning worship service when I saw a young mother and her young daughter having a discussion. I did not recognize the family, and so I stopped, asked their names, and introduced myself. The young mother then said to me, "She does not want to go to the worship service. This is something new for us because she is only six years old." She then pointed to her daughter and said, "She is getting ready for a temper tantrum."

As I stood there for a few minutes, it was obvious that the mother did not know what to do with her daughter. On an impulse I said, "May I talk with your daughter for a minute?" She nodded approval, and I took the little girl aside and explained to her about the experiences to be had in the coming worship service. I then told her a story about growing up without a mother who took me to the church services and how I wished I had had parents with me in church. I then encouraged the little girl to go and participate in the children's sermon time and the other opportunities provided for her and her mother in the service. When we finished talking, the mother thanked me, and the two walked together (with no tantrum) toward the sanctuary.

During the service, I watched for the little girl when the time came for the children's sermon. She walked down the aisle with the other children and then participated with the others in distributing small American flags to all the veterans who were in the service that morning. The little girl smiled as she quickly returned to her mother after the sermon and activity. I was so thankful to have been able to help this family through a temporary struggle with attending the corporate worship service together.

Parent education should begin before the couple's first child is born. This is a vulnerable time in their lives and is a time when they often are looking for all the help they can receive. So many young adults come from dysfunctional homes and did not have strong Christian role models in their family. Simply to tell them *what* the Bible says without telling them *how* to apply its teachings is a mistake. We should be specific and helpful. Deuteronomy 6:6–9 states,

> Parent education should begin before the couple's first child is born.

> These words that I am giving you today are to be in your heart. Repeat them to your children. Talk about them when you sit in your house and when you walk along the road, when you lie down and when you get up. Bind them as a sign on your hand and let them be a symbol on your forehead. Write them on the doorposts of your house and on your gates.

Teaching children is both a challenge and a privilege. Teaching parents of children is both a challenge and a privilege.

Review Questions

1. How do the parents in your church prefer receiving information regarding the children's ministry?

2. What are the most challenging needs of the parents in your church?

3. Have parent education conferences been conducted at your church? If not, are parent education conferences a possibility?

4. Does your church have a children's committee to address ongoing needs in the children's division?

5. Does your children's ministry have a written set of policies that can be provided to parents of children?

6. Has your church provided a training session to make all church members aware of the growing number of child abusers in our society?

Essential #9

LEAD IN PROVIDING FACILITIES AND EQUIPMENT FOR AN ATTRACTIVE LEARNING ENVIRONMENT

By B. J. Cranford, M.A. Religious Education

The physical environment for children in grades 1–6 conveys a message to children and parents. The way a room looks, smells, and feels tells children and parents about the teaching and learning that may or may not happen in the room. Understanding the stages of child development and how those stages are related to the environment is important for creating space that meets the needs of children.[112] A great environment for children provides a safe and stimulating place for children to explore, experience, and understand the world around them through a biblical lens.

How the Physical Environment Influences Learning/ Competency

Children learn as they interact with forces and things in their environment. Learning cannot be imposed from the outside. The children must interact with their world. Learning follows a definite sequence that cannot be hurried by any adult. Creating and implementing a learning environment means careful planning. The physical space of the classroom is managed as the teacher prepares the room for the students. Is the space warm and inviting? Do the children have access to necessary materials? Attending to these and similar questions aids a teacher in managing the physical space of the classroom.

Are the distracting features of a room eliminated? The visual environment may distract children if too many decorations or materials are in the room. A study of kindergarten children found several conclusions that are helpful in designing an environment for children at church, even though this study focused on a school setting. The children were more likely to be distracted by the visual environment when placed in a decorated room. When they were placed in a sparse classroom, they were more likely distracted by their peers or themselves. The room's visual environment affected the amount of time children spent off task, spending more time off task in the decorated room. Learning scores were lower in the decorated room, leading researchers to conclude that the decorated room led to greater time off task and this led to reduced learning.[113]

While the physical learning environment is important for learning, the emotional environment is also important for the spiritual growth in elementary children. It is important for children to feel cared for and loved; to have choices; to have their families included and informed; to have ownership of things happening in the room; and to treat each other with respect and kindness.[114]

124

First Impression Checklist

- Does the area smell clean? Does it look clean and uncluttered?
- Are you and your child warmly welcomed and directed to a class or the worship center?
- Is a secure check-in/pickup system in place for children? Are you given a security card or sticker to pick up your child at the end of the session?
- Are allergy alert posters easily seen if food or nature items are to be used in the session?
- Are at least two adult teachers present in the room?
- Is the room prepared for teaching when the first child arrives?
- Are children greeted by name on entering their room?
- Are the tables and chairs sized appropriately for the age group using the room?
- Are the supplies neatly placed on shelves or counter tops?
- If a bulletin board is in the room, is it up to date and attractively decorated with God-centered themes?
- Are there easy to follow directional signs to the children's area?
- Is the room an adequate size for the number of children in the class? Is there a room arrangement that allows for open space?
- Are the walls free from clutter and painted a soothing color?

Technology in the Children's Room

Technology is everywhere, and children use it daily. A 2010 study by the Kaiser Foundation showed that elementary children use entertainment technology (TV, Internet, video games, computers/tablets, cell phones) on an average of seven and a half hours per day.[115] The American Academy of Pediatrics recommends that elementary-age children spend only one to two hours daily utilizing entertainment technology.[116] While there are great benefits of advanced technology, it is important to look at the potential effects this technology may have on children's physical, psychological, and behavioral health as well as their ability to learn and sustain personal and family relationships[117]

It is important to set guidelines for children and their personal cell phones or tablets that they may bring to church. Many of these children may have a Bible app on their phone

> Technology in the rooms can be of benefit. Consider using PowerPoint occasionally to teach. This visual presentation will appeal to the visual learners in your department.

and will use that instead of a printed Bible. As a teacher, one must model appropriate usage of these portable devices. Videos should be used only for a few minutes (five minutes or less). There are ways to utilize tablets and computers for activities, but these electronic devices should only be tools. Relationships are important to children, and technology may interfere with those relationships at church.

The National Association for the Education of Young Children and the Fred Rogers Center for Early Learning and Children's Media at Saint Vincent's College adopted a position statement clarifying how best to use technology in an early childhood setting. Following are two recommended guidelines:

- Evaluate technology by paying attention to the appropriateness and quality of the content, the child's experience, and the opportunities for co-engagement.
- Provide a balance of activities, recognizing that technology and interactive media can be valuable tools supporting

active, hands-on, creative, and authentic engagement with those around them and the world.[118]

Children's Education Space Guidelines

The location of the children's area, the size of the rooms, and the shape of the room are important considerations for creating the learning environment for children. Children's space that considers the development of the child will foster good teaching. Churches have only one chance to make a first impression. The following guidelines represent the ideal situation, not always the actual situation:[119]

- The children's space should be in a visible part of the church, preferably near the preschool area of the church.
- The entry to the children's area helps to set the tone and make a good impression as well as provide security to the area. This space should look inviting to children and parents.
- The general rule for considering the size of a children's room is twenty-five square feet for every child and adult in attendance. Large, open rooms are preferable to small rooms adjacent to a large assembly area. (See room diagrams in Appendix 2 for adaptation of space.)
- Enrollment ceilings and teacher-to-pupil ratios for grades 1–6
  o Maximum enrollment—twenty-four children
  o Ratio of teachers to children—1:6
- Doors should be solid with a small rectangular window for safety and security and staggered down the hall. The doors should open to the inside of the room. The doors should be thirty-six inches wide.
- The child's needs, comfort, cleanliness, and safety are the factors one should consider when deciding on the type of floor. The floor should be easily cleaned and relatively inex-

pensive to maintain. The floor covering should be moderately light in color and free from bold designs. The floors should be carpet, tile, or a combination of both. The carpet should be commercial, tight-loop, antistatic, stain resistant, and antimicrobial.

- A high-quality and nontoxic paint or vinyl wallpaper is preferred for the walls in the children's area. The color should be a neutral color or a pastel color. The use of bold colors or patterns is discouraged, as it may distract learners. Rooms with quite a bit of natural light should use cool colors while rooms with little natural light should use warm colors.
- Murals are discouraged for use in children's rooms. The permanence of the mural subject will fail to reinforce what is being taught each Sunday, and visuals in a classroom should relate to the current lesson. If a church decides to use some type of mural, it is suggested to avoid putting these in hallways, as this can make a hallway look crowded. A mural could work well at the entry to the children's area.
- Natural light is recommended if possible.
- Ceilings with acoustical tiles and fluorescent lighting are the best choices for use in children's rooms.
- Provide restrooms near the children's rooms.

Furnishings and Equipment

The furnishings and equipment for the children's rooms should enhance the Bible teaching environment. All ministry groups using the children's area will utilize the same furnishings and equipment and must meet the needs of the children using the rooms. Good teaching can take place with minimum supplies and equipment.

Guidelines for Purchasing Furnishings

The furnishings and finishes are the backdrop for the materials and the children using the materials. The focus should be on quality and durability, not on immediate cost savings. Consider the initial cost vs. the lifetime cost of the furnishings. Evaluate what the cost may be to repair an inexpensive piece of furniture and how often it may need to be replaced. It may be more cost effective to purchase high-quality furniture on items that will be used more often. Keep in mind how much the furniture will be utilized, and choose furnishings that can easily be cleaned and will be durable.[120]

Recommended Equipment[121]

- Chairs
    - o Grades 1 and 2—seat is 12–13 inches from floor
    - o Grades 3 and 4—seat is 14–15 inches from floor
    - o Grades 5 and 6—seat is 16–17 inches from floor
- Tables—Tabletops for children should be 10 inches above the chair seats. The minimum dimensions for tables are 30 inches by 48 inches, but the recommended dimensions are 36 inches by 54 inches. Adjustable tables are also recommended.
- Shelves—14–19 inches deep, 42–46 inches high, and 3–4 feet long
- Tack board or bulletin board—Bulletin boards should be 30 inches from the floor.
- Resource cabinet
- CD player
- Coat rack

Optional Equipment

- Sink
- Markerboard
- TV/DVD player—This can be shared by several departments.

General Guidelines for Arranging Classrooms[122]

- Think about the natural flow and traffic patterns in the room. Make space a priority by removing any unnecessary furniture from rooms. Children need room to move. Too many chairs and tables may restrict movement.
- Use all of the space all of the time. Chairs and tables can be moved around the room as needed.
- Chairs and/or rugs can be used instead of tables if space is an issue. Lapboards made of cardboard or plywood can replace tables.
- Teaching materials in each room should relate to the session. Place several Bibles around the room in the various small-group settings.
- Provide easy access from the doorway to the Bible study groups.

Maintaining a Safe Environment

The safety and security of a child should be one of the most important considerations for the children's ministry. Providing a secure children's area with controlled access will put parents at ease with leaving their children with teachers. While many churches cannot provide this secure area, churches can provide security teams to be present in the children's area to help raise the level of security. Training teachers to be aware of their surroundings will help raise the level of security. Training teachers to know what to do in case of a fire, tornado, or earthquake is important. Always provide two adult teachers in each room. Conduct background checks on all teachers of children. Other steps to be taken are:

- Evaluate with your teachers and staff the weak and strong safety areas of your programs.
- Make a plan of action to target specific areas.
- Schedule any training that needs to occur. Organizations such as the local Red Cross, fire department, and law enforcement officials can help with training.
- Use experts in your congregation.
- Notify parents of plans or changes.
- Create a safety manual.

Facility Safety Checklist[123]

Utilize the following checklist to evaluate your current children's area. Make notes of items needing repair or replacement.

- ☐ Protruding nails or other sharp objects
- ☐ Sharp corners or edges on furniture
- ☐ Broken tile or damaged/loose carpeting
- ☐ Peeling paint on walls or furniture
- ☐ Unsecured windows
- ☐ Cluttered hallways
- ☐ Loose rails or steps on stairwell
- ☐ Closets and storage areas that are fire hazards
- ☐ Damaged electrical outlets or fixtures
- ☐ Mold, mildew, or dampness

- ☐ Damaged blinds or shades
- ☐ Unsecured or unstable shelves and/or cabinets
- ☐ Broken chairs or tables
- ☐ Exposed asbestos
- ☐ No fire escape route posted or practiced (The fire department can help.)
- ☐ No first-aid kit available or is understocked
- ☐ Dust is present (allergy sufferers)
- ☐ Damaged or dirty ceiling tiles or light fixtures
- ☐ Obstructed or no glass window in doors

Sharing Space[124]

A coordinated effort will help allocate children's space for all programs that meet at the church during the week. Program leaders should meet at the beginning of the church year to discuss concerns and to cooperate in the use of rooms. Designating cabinet space for the various programs is helpful but not necessary. A general supply cabinet with consumable supplies can be utilized by all programs. Sharing space is easier if the rooms are used by the same age group in each program. Space should be arranged to suit needs for each program using the space.

Communication between all of the programs utilizing the children's space is the key to sharing space. Placing a schedule of room usage and the people responsible for the activities in the room will be helpful, as well as a room arrangement. Assign different walls/bulletin boards to the organizations utilizing the room. Utilize sheets or inexpensive plastic tablecloths to cover items on the wall that are not related to the teaching session. The various children's programs may each have a different focus, but the methods and philosophies of teaching children are the same.

Managing on a Limited Budget

The children's programs of many churches have limited resources and funds. While the resources may be limited, the environment can still be clean and inviting without all the furnishings. The furnishings need to be in good condition, though. Workdays can be scheduled for church members to help repair furniture, paint walls, clean floors, etc. Many supplies can be gathered from church members, reducing the amount of money needed for supplies.

Plan well and as far in advance as possible. Knowing what will be happening six months away can help reduce the cost of items. Purchasing seasonal items during the off season will save money. It is important to keep items organized and labeled, especially if the items will be stored for several months. Centralize the consumable supplies so that all children's departments have access to the supplies. Ordering supplies in bulk will result in savings.

While providing resources for children's rooms is important, remember that the relationships with the teachers and children are most important. Children want to know whether their teachers are going to be there, whether their friends are going to be there, and what activities are planned.

Basic Classroom Resources[125]

- ☐ Bulletin board paper in a variety of colors
- ☐ Dry erase markers and eraser for whiteboards
- ☐ Water-based markers (thin-tip and regular)
- ☐ Crayons
- ☐ Colored art chalk

- ☐ Glue sticks
- ☐ Washable tempera paint
- ☐ Paint brushes (thin & medium tips)
- ☐ Lined paper
- ☐ Manila or white drawing paper (9" x 12" and 12" x 18")
- ☐ Newsprint (9" x 12", 12" x 18", 18" x 24")
- ☐ Typing paper or unlined white paper
- ☐ Crayons
- ☐ Construction paper (9" x 12" and 12" x 18") in various colors
- ☐ Pencils with erasers
- ☐ Scissors (blunt and pointed, child and teacher size, left and right handed)
- ☐ Sentence strip paper with lines
- ☐ Masking tape in a variety of colors
- ☐ Clear tape
- ☐ Rulers
- ☐ Tacks/push pins for bulletin boards/tack strips
- ☐ Hole punches
- ☐ Paper clips
- ☐ Poster board
- ☐ Pencil sharpener (electric if possible)
- ☐ Stapler and staples
- ☐ Bible dictionary for young readers
- ☐ Bible handbook
- ☐ Simple Bible maps
- ☐ Bible timeline
- ☐ Bible atlas for children
- ☐ Extra Bibles
- ☐ Books about life in Bible times
- ☐ Books with photographs of present-day Palestine

Review Questions

1. Why should visual distractions be eliminated from children's rooms?

2. Why is it important to limit the use of technology in the children's environment?

3. What are some of the recommended furnishings for children? How important are these furnishings?

For Further Reading

Fisher, A.V., K. E. Godwin, & H. Seltman (2014). "Visual environment, attention allocation, and learning in young children when too much of a good thing may be bad." *Psychological Science,* doi:10.1177/0956797614533801

Smith, J. *Essentials for Excellence: Connecting Children's Sunday School to Life.* Nashville, TN: Life Way Press, 2003.

Essential #10

DEVELOP SKILLS FOR SECURING, DEVELOPING, MOTIVATING, AND MINISTERING TO CARING LEADERS AND TEACHERS

By Donna B. Peavey, Ph.D.

I have a great passion for laying foundations for faith in children, teaching them God's word, and leading them to love God with all their hearts, souls, and minds. Yet being a children's minister is not just teaching children; it is also enlisting and equipping leaders who work with children and families. As a new church staff member, I learned quickly that I needed to build and maintain a strong team in order to meet the needs of the children and families that God had entrusted to my care.

Securing Body Builders

Like many church leaders, I struggled with finding *the right workers* to build my team. I was looking for people who loved children and had experience teaching them. Who were they? Where were they hiding? I confess that I actually sat on the platform during worship gazing over the congregation looking for people I could approach about serving in the children's ministry. I finally decided to let go and let God do what God does best—meet my needs and the ministry needs for our church. Philippians 4:19 says, "And my God will supply all your needs according to His riches in glory in Christ Jesus" (NASB). God loves his church, children, and their families even more than I do.

God revealed the workers when I relied on God and focused on the right thing—commitment to Christ. Jesus said, "If anyone wants to be My follower, he must deny himself, take up his cross, and follow Me" (Mark 8:34, HCSB).[126] Instead of looking for *the right workers*, I began to look for people committed to following Christ.

> A word *not* used by God to describe a follower of Christ is *volunteer*.

The words found in Scripture that God uses to describe the followers of Christ include *members of a body, disciples, servants, a holy nation,* and *a royal priesthood* (see Ephesians 4:11–13; Matthew 20:25–26; 1 Peter 2:9). I believe that words are important, particularly those used by God. A word *not* used by God to describe a follower of Christ is *volunteer*.

Webster's Dictionary defines a volunteer as a person who undertakes some task or service of his or her own free will.[127] This person is also unpaid. Among other reasons, people volunteer because they want to do something with their time or because they value the work of an organization. In the United States, volunteerism is highly valued and often equated with community service. In fact, the United States Department of Labor tracks the volunteer service of adolescents and adults[128]

Because volunteers serve at their own will, they also control the length and type of their service. Unlike volunteers, disciples of Christ are to deny themselves, submit to service out of obedience, and forsake everything to follow Christ as long as they live (Mark 8:34; Luke 14:33). Therefore, I believe we need to change our focus from enlisting volunteers to enlisting committed Christ-followers—also known as *body builders*.

Scripture tells us, "And He personally gave some to be apostles, some prophets, some evange-lists, some pastors and teachers, for the train-ing of the saints in the work of ministry, to *build up* the body of Christ, until we all reach unity in the faith and in the knowledge of God's Son, growing into a mature man with a stature measured by Christ's fullness" (Ephesians 4:11–13, italics added for empha-sis). In Romans 12:5–6 we read, "In the same way we who are many are one body in Christ and individually members of one another." God has gifted every Christian for service in the work of ministry for the purpose of *building up* and strengthening the body of Christ.

> We need to change our focus from enlisting volunteers to enlisting committed Christ-followers—also known as *body builders*.

Where do you look for children's ministry body builders? Open yourself to cultivate relationships with people you may not have previously considered. Years ago as a young adult serving in chil-dren's ministry, I took a trip with the senior adults to Williamsburg, Virginia. Not only did I have a great time, but I also developed rela-tionships with a group of people with whom I had little contact prior to the trip. Because of our relationship, they were more than willing to serve in the children ministry when asked. Not only did they serve, but they also recruited others.

College students are seeking ways to serve the church and have a great need for fellowship. Using their gifts and abilities to serve in the children's ministry provides them an opportunity to grow as builders and experience the support of a faith community. Students who are unable to return home on a regular basis will appreciate the sense of community forged through service.

Like college students, single adults are seeking fellowship, service, and opportunities for growth. Single adults include the divorced, widows, widowers, those who never married, and every age group. As with other adults in the church, single adults can contribute to the work of the church through service in the children's ministry.

Parents are excellent body builders. They are always on our list and are the people we tend to approach first. Many parents have a passion for serving children and enjoy young children. Some parents may be able to serve for Vacation Bible School or a special event but not commit to a weekly ministry position. Don't assume, though, that all parents want to serve or should serve with children. We need to encourage them to serve in ministries where their gifts and interests can be used best.

Before you begin placing body builders in positions, you need to organize your ministry.

- *Develop a children's ministry vision statement.* Vision "is the picture we have in our mind's eye of the ideal future for specific individuals (such as children)."[129] Make the statement visible to all church members. Include it in ministry position descriptions.
- *Make a list of all available positions.* Include all areas of service—teacher, hall monitor, extended session volunteer, resource room coordinator, VBS director, snack preparer, etc.—to share with prospective children ministry builders. You may be surprised at what appeals to people.

- *Develop ministry position descriptions* (some call these *job descriptions*). A ministry position description informs the body builder of what is expected. It may also be used to evaluate the person's growth as a body builder and team member. A basic ministry position description should contain the vision statement, the position title, a list of specific responsibilities, the supervising person, and the length of service expected.
- *Know how many builders you need.* You will need enough builders to maintain a proper teacher-child ratio and provide support for the ministry.
- *Organize the space.* Clean and declutter the ministry space. People do not like serving in disorganized chaos. The children's ministry space should be neat and have a pleasing smell.
- *Develop a child protection policy* that includes the following recommendations:
  o Make proper selection of people who work with children.
  o Require a six-month waiting period.
  o Use a written job description (also known as ministry position description).
  o Conduct personal interviews.
  o Check references and document responses.
  o Conduct criminal background checks.[130]

Before you approach a potential children's ministry builder, check your attitude. Attitude matters. The children's ministry is vitally important and worthy of the best builders. Wait on the Holy Spirit to reveal the right builder. Recruit only those people who are gifted and qualified for this ministry. I am reminded of the Marine slogan, "The Few. The Proud. The Marines." They are an elite force who exhibit honor, courage, and commitment. Not everyone who applies to be a Marine is accepted.

Being a disciple of Jesus had a high cost, which Jesus made clear. Jesus did not beg anyone to follow him. Follow Jesus' example. Raise the bar for children's ministry builders. Expect more of them. Jesus loves the little children. He said, "But whoever causes the downfall of one of these little ones who believe in Me—it would be better for him if a heavy millstone were hung around his neck and he were thrown into the sea" (Mark 9:42). You are responsible for recruiting people of quality—the best of the best. Don't beg for workers. Public pleas for workers send the message that you will take anyone. You also run the risk of having an unsuitable person volunteer for service. What does this say about your children's ministry? What does this say about your currently serving body builders? What does this say about God? Remember, if anyone will do, then no special gifts or skills are required.

The following comment is a call for an attitude adjustment regarding the recruitment of teachers, and it is applicable to other ministry positions:

> So our first task as recruiters is to remind ourselves what it is we are doing. Recruiters are asking people to share their faith with other Christians. Teaching is a calling and ranked high among the spiritual callings by Saint Paul. To be asked to teach is an honor, and also a challenge. These teachers are going to be given carefully prepared and selected materials to work with and will have the support of the entire church. All of this is being done because the church places a very high value on Christian growth. So, set aside the cloud of doom, and approach the task of recruiting teachers for the church's educational ministry with the prayerful energy it deserves.[131]

Before approaching any potential ministry builder, you need to pray and seek the guidance of the Holy Spirit. The Holy Spirit is very interested in what you are doing. Jerry Stubblefield suggests an enlistment process that I have adapted for use with prospective children ministry builders.

> Before approaching any potential ministry builder, you need to pray and seek the guidance of the Holy Spirit.

Before the meeting:

1. *Pray for the leadership of the Holy Spirit.* Ask God to prepare you and the person to be receptive and responsive to God's leadership.

2. *Make an appointment.* Builders should not be recruited when you are passing them in the hallway or rushed for time. They need to have time to ask questions.

During the meeting:

3. *Present challenges of the position.* Present the position description, requirements for service, and the child protection policy. Tell the person that all ministry applicants must be cleared prior to service. Communicate that the position requires dedication. You want the person to understand that service in this ministry influences the spiritual formation of children and contributes to the work of the church. Scottie May and others propose that as you are speaking with potential ministry leaders, you should invite them to tell you of their ministry dreams.[132]

4. *Be realistic about the position.* Describe the actual amount of time the position requires each week. Teaching requires preparation, not just the one programmed hour. The physical

demands of children's ministry should be communicated. Be truthful. You want builders to trust you.

5. *Describe training opportunities.* The prospective builder should understand that training is provided so effective ministry will take place and that by accepting the ministry position, he or she will be provided opportunities for skill development and spiritual growth.

6. *Ask the prospect to pray and study for a week or two before giving you a decision.* Tell the person you will call in a few days to respond to any questions.

After the meeting:

7. *Call or visit to receive the answer.* If you receive an affirmative answer, then review items 3–5, and assure the person of your support.

8. *Follow up.* Check in with the builder on a regular basis to see how he or she is doing and to provide encouragement and support.[133]

Developing/Equipping Body Builders

Church leaders are not to do all the work for the people but to train and equip them to do the work for themselves, *so that the body of Christ may be built up.* If the body of Christ is to be built up, the saints will have to do it.

Ministry to children can be challenging for a church. What do children's ministry body builders have to learn for effective ministry to happen? What they need to know includes:

- Spiritual development of children
- Roles of the faith community and home in a child's spiritual development
- Biblical models of teaching
- Characteristics of children and appropriate teaching methods
- Health and safety guidelines

Ministry training should be both practical and convenient. One size does not fit all when it comes to equipping body builders. Suggestions for equipping include:

- *Independent study.* Builders can use books, videos, and other resources to develop skills on their own time.
- *Church training events.* Different types of training can be planned to meet the needs of builders.
  - o Enlist a specialist to conduct quarterly training sessions.
  - o Provide workshops for teachers to prepare Bible learning activities.
- *Associational, state convention, and national training events.*
  - o Attend a ministry training conference as a group.
  - o Provide scholarships to cover the cost.
- *Meetings.* Meetings are a natural time to equip builders with ministry skills.
  - o Recommend books or articles for builders to read; in the meeting, review what they have read.
  - o Take your ministry builders on a retreat. Spend time in spiritual reflection as well as skill development.
- *In-service.* Have prospective children's ministry builders serve in training with an experienced builder.

Motivating Body Builders

We want children's ministry builders to be motivated and passionate about serving children and their families. The children's ministry leader plays a significant role in establishing a climate that is positive and fulfilling. Suggestions for creating a climate for motivation include these:

- *Help builders understand how their spiritual giftedness fits into the children's ministry.* Placing body builders in ministry positions that utilize their giftedness leads to increased motivation. Put the right person in the right position. Misplacement leads to demotivation. For example, a builder with organizational skills should organize the resource room.
- *Provide supplies and resources.* Builders become frustrated when the tools needed to accomplish the task are not made available. Keep supplies stocked. Review curriculum for needed materials. Ask children's ministry builders to provide you with a list of needed supplies.
- *Be a model.* Your passion and enthusiasm will be contagious. People will imitate what they see and hear.
- *Be concerned about others.* Empathy is the ability to share another person's feelings. An effective children's ministry leader will act on that understanding and demonstrate compassion. Feel empathy and demonstrate compassion to show genuine concern.

John Maxwell speaks of five influences on motivation that we can apply to children's ministry:[134]

1. *Significant contributions.* People must see that they are contributing in a significant way to the children's ministry and the spiritual formation of children. Encourage current

children's ministry builders to regularly share with others what service in the children's ministry means to them.

2. *Goal participation.* People are more likely to support children's ministry goals when they have had the opportunity to develop them.

3. *Positive dissatisfaction.* People can transform dissatisfaction into effective change. Children's ministry builders know what needs to be done. Listen to them and their suggestions for the enhancement of the ministry.

4. *Recognition.* People want to be recognized and thanked. Showing appreciation is essential for a growing and effective ministry. Simple ways to appreciate builders include phone calls to express thanks, appreciation fellowships or banquets, personal notes, and words of encouragement.

5. *Clear expectations.* People are motivated when they know what to do and have the confidence that they will be successful. Training to equip builders provides them with needed confidence.

Ministering to Body Builders

Lawrence Richards states that "the wise builder seeks to grow close to others, for in the intimacy of shared lives God's building grows."[135] He points out that the building up of the church takes place when we

- *work at maintaining peace and harmony in our fellowship* (Romans 14:19),
- *seek each other's welfare* (Romans 15:2; Matthew 7:12), and
- *love others* (1 Corinthians 8:1; John 13:34).

147

You minister to someone when you meet the person's needs. Opportunities for ministering to builders will become apparent as you serve alongside them. You will have the opportunity to minister in times of great rejoicing, in times of crisis, and in the routines of everyday life. Here are some specific times and ways that you may minister to body builders:

- *Times of celebration (birthday, anniversary, marriage).* Send a card, acknowledge in the ministry newsletter, make a phone call.
- *Illness of a child.* Help with doctor visits, provide child care for siblings, furnish meals.
- *Illness of spouse.* Furnish meals, do grocery shopping, offer child care.
- *Birth/adoption.* Bring gifts for newborn and siblings, supply child care for siblings, furnish meals.
- *Loss of job.* Arrange financial aid, furnish meals or groceries, offer emotional support.
- *Miscarriage.* Offer emotional support, furnish meals, provide support group.
- *Child with special needs.* Provide respite care, provide support groups, help with visits to the doctor or therapist.
- *Divorce.* Listen, offer emotional support, provide support groups for children and adults.[136]

Sometimes we anticipate a time of ministry; that is, we look forward to it. Sheila was a gifted children's teacher and a working single mother struggling to make ends meet. She was determined to earn a GED. Our ministry team supported her and encouraged her as she studied. When she received her diploma, we all celebrated.

Other times of ministry are unanticipated. One of my most poignant times of ministering to a fellow servant came early one morning. I received a call from Maria, a teacher in the church weekday early education program. Her adult handicapped son had died unexpectedly during the night. Adding to her family's grief was their financial situation. They did not have the funds necessary to buy a gravesite and receive the burial and funeral services of a funeral home. Our ministry team went into action. Within a matter of hours, donations were obtained, and the services of a funeral home were secured. This precious servant ministered daily to children. In Maria's time of need she received abundantly from the body of hrist.[137]

In more than thirty years of serving in children and children's ministry, I have been both the ministry leader and the recruited. As a ministry leader, the Lord has taught me that I need to wait on the Lord to reveal the person the Lord has for a ministry position. As the recruited, I have learned to rely on the Lord to reveal the position in which my giftedness will be used best to build up the body of Christ.

Focus on people who need to serve, not on positions that need to be filled. Assist members of the body of Christ in discovering, developing, and demonstrating their spiritual gifts, and you will experience dramatic changes in your children's ministry.

> Focus on people who need to serve, not on positions that need to be filled.

Review Questions

1. What relationships within the body of Christ are you intentionally cultivating?

2. Do you have a motto or slogan? What does it communicate?

3. One of the suggestions for creating a climate for motivation highlighted the necessity of modeling. In what ways do you model your passion and enthusiasm?

4. Walk through the children's ministry space at your church. What do you see and hear? What changes would you make to increase the motivation of children's ministry body builders?

For Further Reading

Blackaby, Henry, and Richard Blackaby. *Spiritual Leadership: Moving People on to God's Agenda*. Nashville: Broadman & Holman Publishing, 2011.

Bozeman, Jeanine, and Argyle Smith. *Interpersonal Relationship Skills for Ministers*. New Orleans: Pelican Publishing, 2004.

Wilkes, Gene. *Jesus on Leadership: Timeless Wisdom on Servant Leadership*. Carol Stream, IL: Tyndale, 1998.

Essential #11

DEVELOPING A VIABLE SYSTEM FOR COMMUNICATING WITH CHILDREN, PARENTS, TEACHERS, AND THE CONGREGATION

By Kristi Williams, Ph.D.

After participating in many salvation-decision counseling sessions with children and their parents, you come quickly to the realization that communication is not an easy matter. I remember a home visit many years ago that was for the purpose of following up with the parent and child about the child's desire to be baptized. "I would like to hear the story of how you became a Christian," began the teacher who accompanied me on the visit. "Oh, it's quite a story," interjected the mother before the child could open his mouth. "One day I was picking him up from school, and as I was waiting in the carpool line, I saw that he stepped off the curb in front of a bus. A teacher was right there and pulled him out of the way just in the nick of time, and that's how he was saved." Yes! Well! All this is a reminder that our communication with children, parents, teachers, and the congregation is a complicated web.

The Need for a Viable System of Effective Communication

The need for a viable system of effective communication with children, parents, teachers, and

> How we communicate with children is a reflection of Jesus' value of children.

indeed throughout the whole congregation begins with *God's design for us to be in relationship with God and with each other*. Effective communication is a reflection of who we are as *image bearers* (Genesis 1:26–27). It is vital for us to understand that how we communicate with children is a reflection of Jesus' value of children, expressed as Jesus welcomed them and blessed them (Matthew 19:13–15).

Basics for Effective Communication

For complete and effective communication to occur, *a message must be both given and received*. If you follow up on a project being completed by an assistant or intern, be wary if the individual reports that he or she has *communicated* solely by depositing a message on the receiver's phone or computer.

Messages often become a personal reflection of a person's character and comportment. A message may be words, images, or even smells and other elements in a purposeful environment. Insist on using spell check to review written communication, but be aware that a separate round of editing will be needed to catch grammatical mistakes. Your message will also include symbolic communication such as *body language*.[138] So, when called on to communicate in a high-pressure situation, practice in front of a mirror to cut down on fidgeting, and write down your message, editing it for brevity.[139]

Messages are received by audiences, each of whom brings his or her own set of elements to the conversation. It is wise to consider how someone with a different background may hear the message you intend to send.

The culture in which you are immersed will have a strong bearing on which communication conventions are valued. Gender, personality types, and generational frames are also highly influential in communication systems. Specialty publications regarding each are readily available (see especially *Communication Plus* and *Leading from Your Strengths* on the "For Further Reading" list at the end of this chapter).

> Be wise, and keep your mind open to understand how effective communication is accomplished in your specific ministry context.

With so many communication options available, and many more likely to come after publication of this text, these principles can assist in developing systems for viable communication:

1. Consider your audience.

2. Choose the mode(s) that will most effectively communicate your message.

3. Repeat your message frequently.[140]

4. Listen and seek feedback.[141]

Tools to Consider for Effective Communication Systems

In your communication systems, more tools are at your disposal than you are likely to realize at the beginning. A hallway conversation may go far in fostering effective communication. "I just have to stop you," said the father as a family passed the children's minister.

"This week my son had a belt test in his karate class. During the session, the instructor reiterated teaching about self-control, discipline, and trust. He asked the class whom they most trusted. Without hesitation my first-grade son raised his hand and was called upon. 'I trust Jesus Christ the most!' answered my son. Now, why I wanted to tell you this was because we are fairly private about belief issues in our home, and so I know that this is something he learned at church. What you are doing makes a difference in our family." View every interaction as a building block in understanding your organization, learn to listen well to people, and experiment with the communication styles and preferences of others.[142]

In an informative comparison of ministry models presented by May, Posterski, Stonehouse, and Cannell, five models are dissected to show "differences among our perceptions and assumptions" that are communicated through each ministry approach.[143] Finding philosophical agreement with one of these metaphors can be a helpful first step in better understanding how to structure effective communication systems.

Curriculum used with children is a tool for communicating the values of an organization. The well-reasoned presentations in *Perspectives on Children's Spiritual Formation* allow a reader to understand how each of four teaching models and subsequent curricular choices communicates different values about how children learn about God and how we experience God.[144] *Tru* curriculum published by David C. Cook is a contemporary elementary-age curriculum that has an integrated plan for communicating a consistent "Big God Story" message to children, teachers, and parents.[145]

In the digital age, the classroom will not be the only venue for communicating a spiritual lesson, as learning continues through electronic media during the week. In addition to thinking about *where* a child is spiritually instructed, "now we must add *when* and *how* as well."[146]

In today's climate a ministry is called on to maximize creativity. If you feel you are lacking in creativity, draft a volunteer who is gifted in this area. Go beyond traditional printed items and consider communication points such as a rotating art gallery exhibit displaying artwork produced by children. Hold on to tried-and-true communication tools such as a personal handwritten note, which has long stood as a testimony to care and attention.

Be sure to include the routine of making regular phone calls as a key element in your communication system. If the sheer volume of calls needed to reach people in your organization is overwhelming, tools such as a phone tree automatic message generator may be helpful.[147]

In many cultures, home visits can still be effective times for connecting with families, if you set your communication goals in advance and show common courtesy by calling ahead. When visiting to follow up with a child's spiritual decision, let the parent know ahead of time what part you want the parent to have in the conversation. Consider taking a variety of resources that a parent can use after you depart. You may find it helpful to role play about possible obstacles and how to overcome those before entering a ew situation.

Sometimes a church-sponsored seasonal event, such as a fall hayride, may be helpful in gathering families from distant neighborhoods. Summer day camps or church-sponsored field trips are another way to purposefully develop fellowship among families, and these events provide a natural two-way communication path between a ministry team, children, and parents.

The popularity of various digital and social communication platforms will continue to rise and fall with the times, and stay-

> The goal of all tools is to make a connection and accomplish communication.

ing current with these tools poses some of the greatest challenges of modern communication. Identify the top two or three ways in which you will choose to communicate most messages, and make it clear—especially to parents, teachers, and colleagues—how they can best receive and return communication with you. Generally, all digital media should be kept up-to-date, and best practices showing how to accomplish the highest communication rate will need to be frequently reviewed.

Communicating with Children

As we communicate with children, it is critical to keep in mind that every day our relationships with children provide them "with experiences that prepare them for faith."[148] The oft-quoted Proverbs 22:6 ("Train a child in the way he should go, and when he is old he will not turn from it," NIV84) dovetails with a comment from Tedd Tripp, that a major objective of communication with children is to understand the child and promote the child to success along the way God has created him or her.[149]

School-age children are moving through a time in which they need affirmation of their contributions in the church setting and affirmation of their personhood. They are critically observing the way role models communicate biblical truths in order to ensure that words match up with actions. This is a developmental age where children can earnestly begin to understand that they are part of the church community if there is a plan for them to be active in various serving roles and projects. On the other hand, a congregation that fully segregates children into age-graded learning environments may find that they are communicating an attitude of "You can be part of the church when you grow up!"[150]

Effective communication systems need to consider the messages that should be directed to children. First, consider messages that uphold the church and parent communication partnership—messages that reinforce what parents should be communicating with their children as they rise up, as they lie down, and as they walk along life's way (see Deuteronomy 6:7).[151] Second, under the direction of the Holy Spirit to guide the continual development of a ministry framework, consider messages that uphold the core values of your ministry.[152] Third, consider messages that purposefully move children forward in their development and understanding of spiritual matters. Many publishers issue a scope and sequence document pointing to the communication goals of their curriculum.

School-age children continue developing foundations for understanding spiritual truths, and some are making personal decisions for heart and life transformation during phases that Art Murphy names the Discerning Stage, the Deciding Stage, and the Discipling Stage.[153] In support of children and their parents, seek helpful resources such as articles and workbooks that are in agreement with your church's denominational or theological perspective, especially ones that can be loaned out or distributed to families that are processing through issues, such as salvation and baptism, with their young children. Not all aspects of salvation are connected with the communication of facts, and a brief spotlight on three key salvation issues can be found in the book, *Nurture That Is Christian*.[154]

Although the core essence of children has not changed, it has often been said that *childhood*

> Stories are communication tools for capturing a child's heart and mind through imagination.

has changed. One comparison of the change is to consider aspects of language and communication in the *modern* era compared with society's move into a *postmodern* era.[155] In a world of ever-increasing technology and creative stimuli, those who work with children are prompted to make sure they seek always to teach children, to teach them God's ways, and to teach in creative ways.[156] Most often, teaching children the Bible will still involve communicating through story, an age-old method for capturing a child's heart and mind through imagination.[157] Guidelines for telling a Bible story in an engaging manner can be found in Dunlop's volume, *Follow Me as I Follow Christ*.[158]

Special events can be an effective tool for communicating with elementary and preteen children. Younger children are not fully independent in their social relationships, and events targeting these age groups may need to include parents, or at least a low ratio of chaperones to students.

Overnight camps for the older age groups who are deepening social relationships with peers can be an extremely effective way to focus on teaching spiritual truths in a unique venue. An effective strategy is to reserve some activities in your program calendar for specific age groups so that children look forward to what is ahead. A weekend retreat for preteens in their last year of children's ministry is used effectively by many churches to set student expectations for the upcoming year and to aid in the transition to a youth ministry department.

Communicating with Parents

Two-way communication from a ministry leader to parents is a key component in a viable and efficient system of communication. This communication should help align parents with the ministry trajectory, seeking to include them as full-fledged partners.

What do parents need to hear from you? First, communicate expectations that you have for them, and in turn, communicate what a parent can expect from your ministry.[159] Second, practice communication that builds good community relations. Third, include parents as you celebrate successes, for everyone wants to be on a winning team. Fourth, include parents in communication about the specific needs that exist in the children's ministry department.

Perhaps most importantly, parents need communication that trains them to be godly parents

> Parents need communication that trains them to be godly parents.

who are equipped to raise their children to love the Lord and to uphold true ministry partnership between home and church.[160] In ministry that is structured to partner with parents in the home, it makes sense to reinforce consistent messages.[161] In the cases where parents are not already firmly established in communicating Christ-centered character and spiritual transformation messages to their children, age-group specialists and ministerial staff can help by disseminating intentional and memorable messages in tools that parents can use in the home.[162] (In addition to curriculum options on the market, a contemporary example of customizable and reproducible resources available to assist churches in communicating topical training to parents can be found at www.drivefaithhome.com. Accessed 9/2/14.) Small-group studies on parenting topics are often popular communication strategies to which parents respond.[163] Use seminars about popular trends, and consider capitalizing on natural development milestones such as the preteen years and transitioning to middle school to gain the attention of parents.

Communicating with Parents in Crisis

Parents and children are not always living in the ideal situations that we would wish for them. In the children's ministry context, common crisis scenarios tend to be repeated: behavior issues, health issues, complications related to atypical development, etc. As you begin growing in maturity and experience as a children's ministry leader, share the burden of these times with others who can give confidential wise counsel to avoid land mines.

A children's ministry associate with responsibilities for the program providing services for children with special needs was approached with an unexpected crisis. One Sunday a parent arrived at the self-contained classroom for children with special needs and declared to the teacher that this would be her son's last day in the class. The parent had found a buddy to accompany the child to a typical classroom, and the parents were ready to move forward with that solution. What was the crisis? The associate knew that the typical classrooms were not equipped to assimilate this child and buddy without some coaching and development. The parent went into crisis mode because she was hurt that her child couldn't immediately be placed in a classroom with typically developing children.

Together with an experienced mentor, the associate arranged a conference with the parents as soon as possible to seek a win-win solution for all involved. Here are some of the strategies they employed:

1. Seek a noncrisis time to have an even-keeled conversation about the issue.

2. Uphold the authority of a parent and respect his or her child. (Do not discuss a crisis involving the child in front of the parent or in front of other uninvolved parties.)

3. Listen carefully and clarify the crisis among all involved parties.

4. Affirm the areas of agreement between the children's ministry and the parent.

5. Outline the areas of disagreement so both parties can understand the true matter to be resolved.

6. If possible, agree on a shared outcome (a goal both parties can seek).

7. Promise to take action, but don't promise a solution over which you do not have full control.

8. Report back to the parent with progress.

9. Follow the path of resolution as far as you can.

Communicating with Children's Ministry Leadership

Your ministry team needs clear communication from you. To effectively multiply your efforts and avoid being a lone-ranger leader, you need to communicate clearly the framework by which others should make organizational decisions. Clear communication from a leader establishes the framework to empower others to make decisions. Jim Wideman uses the term "pushing authority down," and clear communication is key to empowering other leaders so they will know they also have responsibility to accomplish communiction.[164]

Clear communication is needed for alignment among your team. Larry Fowler draws a contrast between communicating as a cowboy or as a shepherd. As their leader, your team needs for you to call to them to follow you in a clear path. They will need encouragement, but after the first few start to follow your communication, momentum will push others toward the vision also.[165]

> Clear communication from a leader establishes the framework to empower others to make decisions.

Clear communication is needed for motivation among volunteers and also among paid staff. Some team members will find motivation when you communicate with them during decision-making processes, and yet others will be energized when you present a challenge for them to conquer.[166] If you get stuck in a rut when it comes to encouraging your team, review a summary of the personality styles and the preferred communication modes of each to gain new perspectives on how to balance out your affirmations to other personalities on the team.[167]

You have probably already noticed that in most established ministry organizations, the children's leadership team and volunteers are not a homogenous group. When you reach a time when you feel that communication is not getting through, take a few minutes and make a list of the various niches represented by your team. You are likely to see opportunities for new communication strategies. One year an established children's ministry took time for an exercise like this and realized that they had a record number of veteran teachers who had not been recognized for their long years of service. To celebrate and share this story with others in the congregation, all teachers who had served five years or longer were recognized with a blue ribbon. Each felt affirmed and blessed by the special recognition that was communicated through simple blue ribbons.

Although you will repeat many things, the hope is that each year will bring growth in your communication plan. Here is a helpful framework to start with when communicating to team members:

1. Set expectations for each side.[168]

2. Clarify key policies and procedures.[169]

3. Value your team and celebrate successes.[170]

4. Establish two-way communication and express interdependence.[171]

Jesus preached to masses and also focused on twelve disciples. It is likely that you will also need to strategize regarding how to spend your time and efforts when it comes to communication with your team. Although each of these strategies is a tried-and-true tool, when obstacles to communication arise, guide your team to embrace new efforts—even new organizational structures—to better get your message across.

Capitalize on opportunities for face-to-face communication, including hallway conversations, power lunches, lunch meetings, interviews, evaluations, and participation in the work of events. (For assistance in outlining a staff meeting agenda for productive communication, consider guidelines from Anthony and Estep.[172])

The frequency of team meetings is likely to vary from weekly (for paid staff) to once or twice a year for the complete volunteer team. When you are with team members, remember that your unspoken presence speaks as loudly as your words. Such times are great opportunities to show what is in your heart.[173]

Digital communication is necessary for most ministries, but be cautious about full reliance on these tools (e-mail, texting, etc.), as there will be slow adopters or team members with limited access. Download centers used for posting curriculum and training materials (RightNowMedia, YouTube, Vimeo, etc.) are beneficial because they empower team members to get resources at their own convenience rather than relying on you, but be sure to guard against copyright infringement in using these tools.

Communicating with the Congregation

A congregation needs to hear from all different parts of the *body*. Through your communication, you are building the story for why things are blessed or why the department may need ore resources.[174]

Start by believing that the congregation is your largest group of supporters. If you have successfully built relationships

> Communicating stories about successes in children's ministry is a key to overcoming "invisibility."

with children, with parents, and with volunteers, keep building on that foundation. Each demographic in the congregation has differing time, talent, or treasure with which to bless children, and so be sure to communicate opportunities for all to be involved. Offer multiple entry points for volunteers to get involved.

Your congregation needs to hear messages that balance the successes of the ministry area with remaining needs. When recruiting due to a critical lack of volunteers, maintain a positive tone by focusing on the success that a large number of children are attending. Guard against negativity of pressure from guilt.

Congregations also need to hear messages that support the diversity found in the church family. Communication tools (verbal, print, photos, videos, and more) should be screened to ensure accurate representations of the true racial mix, age groups, marital statuses, and socioeconomic statuses of which the congregation is comprised. Take time to purposefully communicate support for families that include children with atypical development, letting them know that they are welcomed by your church family.

In many church settings, the safe, secure, and age-appropriate ministry setting for children also isolates this group so that it is out of sight and out of mind to the congregation, which discourages effective communication. Janice Haywood offers ten practical suggestions to overcome "invisibility."[175] Take advantage of any presentation time that is offered, for even presenting a children's sermon or giving the welcome and announcements during a worship service exposes the congregation to children's ministry leadership.

Communicating within the Church Organization

As mentioned, each congregation and ministry has cultural and organizational differences to which a leader must pay attention. Although churches are living organisms and should be directed under godly leadership, the reality is that formal corporate gatherings of individuals also have some characteristics shared by businesses.

First, churches have structures of organizational leadership. Even with a goal for mutual support and equality, each leadership position has different responsibilities.[176] Jim Wideman points to upper leadership as the most important group to receive your communication.[177] The children's minister has different responsibilities than the senior pastor does, but it is critical to pay attention to the organizational structure in your context. Further, it is wise to garner support from multiple positions, especially when change is on the horizon.

Second, churches have decision-making processes, and you will need a clear understanding of the timelines for these processes so you can plan for appropriate communication. In a small church, decisions regarding program and budget matters may regularly be decided by the full congregation. In larger churches, a proposal may need to be submitted to a committee before being transferred to an executive team for approval.

Third, churches have recognized communication channels, and they may not match the organizational chart. Continually look for advocates to spread appropriate messages. Whenever you have an opportunity to communicate with the senior pastor and other volunteers, tell them about the good things happening in children's ministry. In the words of Jim Wideman, "I talk about fruit. I talk about what God is doing. I talk about the God stories and tell the good that is happening."[178]

A leader is called on to communicate three main categories of messages within an organization. First, leaders communicate about change. When guiding change, it is always good to remember to keep communicating even after you are tired of the message, because it is likely that many still have not truly received the communication.[179]

Second, leaders communicate in preparation for and during crisis. Have a well-documented safety plan, including evacuation procedures, to equip the children's ministry leadership team for communicating in an emergency. A security plan that includes procedures for screening volunteers who work with minors should also outline protocol for communicating during a public relations crisis such as abuse allegations.

Third, leaders should proactively communicate for continuity and succession. When you or a program director no longer fill a spot on the organizational chart, your communication track record is likely to have a great impact on the ministry. This is also true for director-level volunteers, positions that are likely to turn over with periodic frequency. A handbook of compiled policies and procedures is a communication tool that is proven to benefit continuity.[180] Such a document serves to clarify the framework in which a ministry operates.

It may seem mundane, but organizational reports can be effective communication tools within an organization if used wisely. Through a blend of data and anecdotal evidence in a budget proposal, you can communicate about the accomplishments and specific needs of your department and also articulate the goals that additional allocations will help you accomplish.

A formal process of personnel evaluations is another tool for communicating with people outside of your department, such as an upper manager, or an oversight body like the budget committee or church council. In a personnel report, hopefully there are successes to brag about and few behavior corrections to report. An annual cycle allows for communication about additional personnel that are requested. (If your organization needs to improve the communication that occurs during a cycle of personnel evaluations, a listing of pertinent issues is included in a volume of Group Publishing's *Volunteer Leadership Series*.[181])

Conclusion

The communication web spun in children's ministry is one of the challenges that makes ministry rewarding. Each interaction is an opportunity for Christ's love and grace to show through us. This arena is one where we directly see God's work and evidences of God's plan come to life right before our eyes because it is a direct connection to relationships. Although we are all *on the way*, it is exciting to travel together in fellowship and in relationships in which we are constantly being molded into the believers God wants us to become. May you be blessed as you continue to develop systems and implement creative strategies for effective communication so that children will be affirmed, parents will be empowered, kingdom workers will be developed, and congregations will be multiplied as we continue fulfilling the Great Commandment (Matthew 22:36–39) and the Great Commission (Matt. 28:19–20) throughout the world.

Review Questions

1. What does communication through the *ministry of presence* look like in your setting? Are there recent wins that you would like to share? If not, how can you make yourself more present in the moment to allow for deeper communication with children, parents, and teachers?

2. Consider your program calendar. Are you intentionally communicating the core values of your ministry through events? Which age groups could benefit from communication opportunities that might be found in new events or programs?

3. Describe a crisis situation in which you attempted to practice good communication. What elements of your communication went awry? What elements were well received? What elements of the communication were under your control? Briefly outline how the given suggestions for communicating in crisis might allow you to have improved communication in a future crisis.

4. Your organizational structures should include tools for communicating about spiritual truths, mission and core values, and strategies for development and growth. Which audiences readily come to mind as you think about each of

these areas of communication? Talk with a friend about the actions you want to take for improvement with at least one audience.

5. How is your communication style (or skill set) challenged by the way your current ministry setting functions more like an organization than a living organism? How is it challenged by the way your current ministry functions more like an organism than a structured organization? What areas of personal growth does this help you identify? For what areas of organizational change do you need to start planning?

For Further Reading

Capps, Todd. *I'm a Christian Now (Older & Younger Kids editions)*. Nashville, TN: LifeWay Christian Resources, 2003.

Haywood, Janice. "Does Communication Flow among Staff, Parents, and Teachers in all Ministries, as well as in the Congregation?" In *Enduring Connections: Creating a Preschool and Children's Ministry*, 61–68. Danvers, MA: Chalice Press, 2007.

Jutila, Craig. "The Big Balancing Act: Communication." In *The Growing Leader: Healthy Essentials for Children's Ministry*, 101–116. Loveland, CO: Group Publishing, 2004.

Levels of Biblical Learning. Nashville, TN: LifeWay Press, 2013. View or download from http://s7d9.scene7.com/is/content/LifeWayChristianResources/Levels-Of-Biblical-Learning-All-2013pdf. Accessed 8/21/2014.

Littauer, Marita, and Florence Littauer. *Communication Plus: How to Speak So People Will Listen.* Ventura, CA: Regal Books, 2006.

May, Scottie, Beth Posterski, Catherine Stonehouse, and Linda Cannell. "Metaphors Shape Ministry." In *Children Matter: Celebrating Their Place in the Church, Family, and Community,* 3–25. Grand Rapids, MI: Wm. B. Eerdmans Publishing Co., 2005.

Tooker, Eric, John Trent, and Rodney Cox. *Leading from Your Strengths: Building Close-Knit Ministry Teams.* Nashville, TN: B&H Publishing Group, 2004.

Tripp, Tedd. "Embracing Biblical Methods: Communication; Types of Communication; and A Life of Communication." In *Shepherding a Child's Heart,* 73–102. Wapwallopen, PA: Shepherd Press, 1995.

Wideman, Jim. "Communicating Your Structure." In *Stretch: Structuring Your Ministry for Growth,* 117–128. Murfreesboro, TN: An Infuse Publication, 2011.

Essential #12

MOTIVATE TEACHERS AND PARENTS

by Bernard M. Spooner, Ph.D.

Some studies indicate that people typically function at about 20 to 30 percent of their potential. These same studies suggest that the difference in organizations that go forward and those that basically are stagnant depends on the ability of leaders to tap additional potential of followers by using quality motivation. In some of the most outstanding organizations, workers may perform at a level of 80 to 90 percent of their potential. Few people or organizations ever achieve the last 10 to 20 percent of their potential.[182]

Percentage of worker potential utilized	Churches that utilize this level of worker potential
80–100	Few churches achieve this percentage of worker potential.
20–80	Many churches achieve this range of worker potential.
0–20	The typical church or organization utilizes this level of worker potential.

Reginald McDonough presented the above chart about percentage of worker potential utilized and four keys to effective motivation in his book *Keys to Effective Motivation*.[183] He identified these keys: *Stability, Teamwork, Affirmation,* and *Challenge*. These indeed are excellent guideposts.

Leaders have much to do with the effectiveness and level of progress in their churches. Developing good leadership is a life-long growth experience. It requires careful attention to the process of leadership development and to being purposeful in the task at hand.

While teaching an evangelism class at New Orleans Seminary, I asked Dr. Richard Jackson to speak to the class. At the time, he was pastor of North Phoenix Baptist Church in Phoenix, Arizona, and was on campus to present the annual evangelism lectures in chapel. I gave him several questions to answer for the class, the first being, "How did you get the church moving into its pattern of evangelism?" As I heard him share his thoughts, it occurred to me that all pastors are not equally gifted in leadership. Most are gifted with deep convictions, which they must communicate to those they seek to lead. Obviously, he is an extremely gifted leader. What appears easy for him must be learned by most of us through applying skills of motivation and leadership.

> Each of us wants to be the best leader and motivator we can be as we serve God.

God does not expect us to function in the same abilities as others as we lead, encourage, and motivate church workers. He does, however, give us our gifts and opportunities for leadership. Good stewardship is becoming the leaders God has gifted us to be. Unless we have a workable understanding of who we are, we may become discouraged as we observe an exceptionally gifted person.

Jesus Demonstrated the Need for Servant Leadership

In Matthew 20:26–28 Jesus was contrasting the poor leadership of that day to what the disciples were being asked to do when he said, "Not so with you. Instead, whoever wants to become great among you must be your servant, and whoever wants to be first must be your slave—just as the Son of Man did not come to be served, but to serve, and to give his life as a ransom for many" (NIV84).[184] In the account in the Gospel of John of the evening meal before Jesus' crucifixion, Jesus demonstrated servant leadership as "he got up from the meal, took off his outer clothing, and wrapped a towel around his waist. After that, Jesus poured water into a basin and began to wash his disciples' feet, drying them with the towel that was wrapped around him" (John 13:4–5). He said a few verses later, "I have set you an example that you should do as I have done for you" (John 13:15).

Practical Motivation Principles

Motivate by leading people to have beliefs and convictions.

Manipulation is not servant leadership, and shallow motivation will not last. A strong biblical foundation of beliefs will last throughout all of life, however. The pastor and

The pastor and others who lead in the church must be certain they are providing the biblical and theological bases for all they ask staff or laypeople to do.

others who lead in the church must be certain they are providing the biblical and theological bases for all they ask staff or laypeople to do. What do we need to teach the workers?

- *Teach members and leaders that they do not work for or serve the pastor, the staff, the Sunday School director, or others.* While our leaders are to be honored and appreciated for their ministry among us, all of us are serving God in the work of God's kingdom. Jesus reminded the disciples of this principle when he said, "Ask the Lord of the harvest, therefore, to send out workers into his harvest field" (Matthew 9:36). There may be times when we may be disappointed in our leader for some good or sometimes misunderstood reason. At those times we must remember that God's work must supersede any thoughts we may have that grow out of such disappointments. We are all serving God.

- *Teach believers an understanding of the nature and mission of the church.* Leadership in churches is involved in mobilizing laypeople or staff members to carry out the various functions of the church: *evangelism, equipping, ministry,* and *worship.* The Scriptures clearly teach that the nature of the church is to carry out these essential functions. If any one of these functions is missing from church ministry, the church becomes imbalanced and suffers in its overall effectiveness. Without evangelism, a church will die; without ministry, the integrity of the church is lost; without equipping people, they may be unable to function well; and without worship and prayer, the church will have little unity or fellowship.

- *Teach the basic beliefs of the Christian faith as given in Scripture and related to the plight of lost people.* The pastor's role is especially important in teaching Christian beliefs and the need for people to know Jesus Christ as Redeemer.[185]

- *Help believers understand they are to be servants and ministers of Christ.* The pastor is the primary equipper of the leadership, but the pastor is equipping leadership to do Christ's ministry through the church (see Ephesians 4). Beliefs and convictions are powerful motivating forces. Our belief needs to be centered on a loving God whose love and grace compel us to love others into God's kingdom. Always be aware that followers are carefully observing their leaders to determine the depth of their convictions.

Communicate a clear vision.

All of us want to be a part of something that is important, meaningful, and successful. Few of us are really happy being a part of something that has little value, seems to be going nowhere, or has little promise of being successful. Jesus gave us his vision for ministry as he instructed the disciples in the Great Commission (Matt. 28:19–20). It is up to the pastor, staff, and lay leaders to join Jesus' vision as it is applied in their local community.

going nowhere, or has little promise of being successful. Jesus gave us his vision for ministry as he instructed the disciples in the Great Commission (Matt. 28:19–20). It is up to the pastor, staff, and lay leaders alike to join Jesus' vision as it is applied in their local community. A clear vision that is well communicated helps the church to move in a Christ-honoring direction.

When church leaders clearly communicate a vision and are acting on that vision, motivation has an added dimension that builds excitement and response across the leadership ranks and to the congregation as a whole. Proverbs 29:18 declares, "Where there is no vision, the people perish" (KJV). A vision describes a future picture of the church or the Sunday School. What would you like to see your church become under the leadership of Christ?

A volunteer children's teacher needs a vision for reaching young children in the community. Teachers must desire the opportunity for children to grow up in the nurture and care of parents who know our Lord Jesus Christ. When the pastor, staff, and volunteer leaders have a clear vision for the future, individual workers begin to see their part in God's vision for the life, work, and ministry of the church.

While serving at the Travis Avenue Baptist Church in Fort Worth, Texas, I saw this principle work in many ways. Laypeople were suggesting and starting new ministries. Members were volunteering to serve. The church began to experience a surge of growth and new levels of evangelism and ministry.

During this time, Don Long and his family joined the church, and he soon appeared at my office to offer to serve somewhere in the life of the church. He said he was ready to go to work and indicated he would serve anywhere he was needed in the life of the church. Within a few weeks, he began teaching in the Student Career Department and soon returned to introduce his new outreach leader to me. Don said, "We have come to tell you that you have done everything you can do to help our class. You have given us an outstanding department director, a classroom, chairs, a table, a list of members, and prospects. If we fail, it won't be your fault. It's our responsibility to build our class and to reach this age group for Jesus Christ." By the end of that church year, the class had gone from six in attendance to twenty-five to thirty people each Sunday. Don caught his own vision and shared it with his group. He caught the vision of the church and was excited and energized to have a part in it. *Vision is essential to good motivation.*

Involve the membership in vision development and in planning.

Often staff members believe laypeople are too busy to be available for vision development and planning. Such a process does take time for all involved, including the pastor and the laity, but it is essential for the highest level of motivation and effectiveness. A small group of eight to fifteen people may serve on a vision planning team, but leaders should give the entire congregation opportunities for input. This process builds the congregation's expectation and anticipation for possible changes and new approaches to be developed and used in the days ahead. We are more likely to claim ownership and give support when we are involved.

Teach and develop a theology and culture of serving.

Good leadership and good motivation help to move people from being spectators to being servants for Christ. Rick Warren of the Saddleback Church in Lake Forest, California, has identified and defined several categories of people in the church. He leads the church staff and key laypeople in a process of moving each person from the outer circles of involvement to the inner core of involvement.[186] The ministry of the church staff and key laypeople is focused on these targeted parts of the congregation. The ultimate goal is that every believer will have his or her own ministry through the church.

In my own experience I have categorized those who participate in the church in four groups: *core leadership, peripheral leadership, active participants, and peripheral participants.* These groups may be described as follows:

1. *Core leadership.* These are the people who actively participate as leaders. They participate in the worship services and respond readily to whatever the church is undertaking. Most give a tithe of their income to the church and support the pastor and staff on a continual basis.

2. *Peripheral leadership.* These are leaders who respond to the bigger issues in the church and relate primarily to the

pastor or key people. They may serve as Sunday School teachers, committee members, or deacons. However, they do not participate fully in all of the basic activities of leadership. They may teach but do not participate in training events or seldom participate in outreach or planning meetings. They may serve on committees, but they do little more in the life of the church than give, perhaps even tithe. However, if a special event is sponsored and the pastor makes a personal effort toward these individuals, they are likely to respond.

3. *Active participants.* These are people who attend Sunday morning worship and Sunday School with a high degree of regularity. They may be active as class officers and participate in special projects of the church, but they are not willing to serve in leadership roles. Some might have served faithfully in the past, but due to family problems or difficulties in the church have become participants only and do not contribute fully in church life.

4. *Peripheral participants.* These are members who attend less than once a month. They may participate in special seasonal events around Thanksgiving, Christmas, or Easter. They may attend worship or Sunday School, but they seldom attend both. If these people are to be involved in the church, it will usually take a special effort on the part of the pastor to attract their attention and participation.

How do you categorize your church's members? These descriptions are listed simply for the purpose of discussion.

The question is, *how can each of these groups be motivated and led to an increased level of participation, involvement, and service for Christ?* If we focus on them and challenge them, they may be moved to higher levels of ministry and greater stewardship of their lives in the work of Christ. Consider these thoughts about focusing on them and challenging them to increased participation and service.

The pastor and staff need to preach and teach the biblical truth that every believer is gifted for

The pastor and staff need to preach and teach the biblical truth that every believer is gifted for service.

service. The pastor could preach a series of messages that speaks to this issue. The pastor might also challenge every believer to participate in a gifts assessment plan designed to help them explore and discover their gifts.

One-time service projects that can be done on a given day can be promoted by Sunday School leaders and have been proven to involve many for the first time. Such a beginning experience may show adults and youth that there is something they can do. A good experience in one project may be all that is needed by some. Some churches conduct such things as a letter writing campaign, Thanksgiving dinner in a disadvantaged area, Vacation Bible School neighborhood pre-enrollment, or a wild game banquet. What possible projects are appropriate for your congregation?

Seasonal Motivational Events for Key Leaders

Many churches launch the Sunday School and fall program in August or early September. This is a special time when new ideas are implemented, new workers are put in place, special training events are held, and good attendance day may be emphasized. All of these help to get the Sunday School or small-group ministries launched. As the fall progresses, however, Thanksgiving and the Christmas holidays come along, and things may seem to wind down to a much slower pace. *What can be done to rekindle the spirit of early fall when the year was launched?*

Most churches function in three seasons of the year rather than four quarters. While a high level of motivation may be difficult to sustain over all twelve months of the year, a *season lift* event before each season—fall, spring, and summer—can help.

1. *Before fall*

Sometime in August, plan a fellowship meal or cookout with all the Sunday School workers or all the department directors (in a larger church). A two- to three-hour event with a meal and a time of planning is usually effective (Friday evening or Saturday morning). Spouses are invited to attend with the Sunday School workers. After the meal (about forty-five minutes), the Sunday School director and/or minister of education (in larger churches) can share a review of the previous year, including a statistical report, progress on any special projects, and other accomplishments of the year. Follow this by announcing church-wide plans already in place for the coming year. The Sunday School director and/or pastor (or minister of education in a larger church) may then share some possible plans for Sunday School/small groups to be considered for the new year. It should be understood that *these are ideas and can be changed* as the group discusses them and chooses to adjust them. (Note: This kind of event can be used by a single age group as well as for all age groups together.)

It is best to offer *some* plan rather than *no* plan, but it is also essential to give the leadership an opportunity to adjust or improve the plan in certain ways. Otherwise, they may feel the new plan is something that has been forced on them. Consequently, without this involvement, you may have much less participation by the leadership in supporting *any* plans. Leaders should focus on the *whats* and give great latitude in determining the details of the *hows*. For example, there are many ways to train workers for Sunday School. It is more important *that* people are trained (a *what*) than *how* they are trained.

Also, it is good to identify other areas that need improvement. Workers may be grouped to discuss approaches to accomplishing various tasks.

If possible, the pastor should be involved in this meeting. The pastor should bring closure to the meeting and lead in prayer after listening carefully to all the proceedings. When church-wide plans for the coming year are discussed, the pastor may give input and share information. The pastor may want to share information about the stewardship emphasis, an evangelistic season that is planned, or other items such as Thanksgiving and Christmas plans. The very presence of the pastor adds importance to this work and shows the pastor the heartbeat of the Sunday School Bible study ministry. From this experience the pastor will gain valuable insight for leading and giving encouragement through preaching, personal leadership in committees, and in other work of the church. Every effort is needed to ensure the pastor is in attendance. The Sunday School desperately needs the pastor's involvement, interest, and service as pastor.

2. Before spring

A meeting similar to the *before fall* event should be conducted in January or early February. The agenda is similar to the *before fall* meeting and should include a progress report of the fall, goals reached, and activities conducted. This event is a checkup and relaunch event. If plans were made in the fall to be carried out in the spring or summer, these should be reviewed as a part of this event. Greater details are now shared as the spring begins. Brainstorming

181

groups may be used to discover new possibilities for addressing one or more areas of need. At times it is wise to appoint a work group to explore possibilities for addressing particular problems. The work group could report in a few weeks.

As the year has progressed, various issues or possibilities may have arisen that can bring excitement for the spring. This meeting is a time of maximizing such possibilities, encouraging the workers, and involving them in plans for the coming season. Care should be taken to ensure that whatever the plan, it is decided on by consensus and/or common commitment.

3. *Before summer*

The *before summer* event should be held in late April or early May before school is out and people begin taking summer vacations. We can encourage people

> Good worker involvement in the planning process helps to bring about a sense of progress and more effective results for the kingdom of God.

to have good vacations and at the same time enable their groups to have positive, quality experiences every Sunday during the summer season.

Again, the agenda for this meeting is similar to the previous seasonal meetings, but it also can be used as a time to begin developing an outline of plans for the fall and the coming year. We review the progress for the first and second seasons of the year and specifically project plans for the summer. We discuss and address any special issues or problems that need to be corrected, improved, or resolved. Finally, the pastor brings closure to this meeting with words of encouragement and support.

Giving Deserved Recognition

Everyone from the youngest child to the oldest and most sophisticated adult needs recognition and affirmation. Recognition may be given through actions as simple as calling a person by name or sending notes at special times, such as birthdays and anniversaries.

We need to be aware also when people are being recognized for special accomplishments and to join in that recognition. Some time back, I read in the *Dallas Morning News* of a waiter, Paul De la Torre, who has worked in one restaurant for four decades. Paul often waits on others and me at lunch. He always gives excellent service and is eager to make the meal a pleasant experience. I clipped the article and presented it to him the next time I went to the restaurant. As I presented it to him, I received a broad smile. Imagine how much affirmation he experienced because of this deserved recognition. I too wanted to contribute to his sense of having made a difference for many people.

Here are some other possibilities for giving deserved recognition:

- Write personal notes commending people for their faithfulness to Christ when they have done something outstanding.
- Express commendation and appreciation publicly.
- Walk through the teaching areas on Sunday morning or during an event to let people know you are interested.
- Give certificates and mementos.
- Conduct an appreciation banquet.
- Give a "Teacher of the Year" award.
- Conduct special commitment services.

Of course, the pastor should be involved in the commitment service and should be asked to participate in some of the suggestions listed above. For example, Dr. James E. Coggin, with whom I served at the Travis Avenue Baptist Church, Fort Worth, would walk through the entire Sunday School a number of times each year. An attitude of support, commendation, and gratitude on the part of the leaders reminds workers of the significance of their ministries in God's kingdom work.

Conclusion

Servant leadership and good motivation go together. It is a joy to serve with leaders who have integrity and learn to build a team of church workers who enjoy serving Christ through Christ's church.

Servant leadership and good motivation go together.

To close this chapter, I have chosen to share a list of practical steps for "Succeeding in Church Leadership" provided by Don Cannata, who served churches in Texas and Alabama for fifty years prior to his retirement. This list reflects the wisdom of experience and excellent leadership skills.

1. Master the planning process:
    a. Objectives
    b. Needs
    c. Priorities
    d. Goals
    e. Actions

2. Stay focused. Church staff work is a job of interruptions.

3. Be proactive in dealing with conflict.

4. Appear confident, friendly, and approachable.

5. Speak first, and learn people's names.

6. Work within the church organization and polity.

7. Follow the democratic process.

8. Be inclusive in your work rather than exclusive.

9. Be open to suggestions from church leaders and members.

10. Avoid taking sides in church conflicts so that you can remain the minister to everyone.

11. Discuss major programs and proposals you are recommending first with the pastor and then with appropriate leaders to assure their support.

12. Accept the fact that much of your success depends on enlistment of the appropriate leaders and committee members.

13. Stay ahead of the learning curve in your field by being informed of the latest trends in your field and by attending professional development clinics and seminars.

14. Discover your particular spiritual gifts, and develop them. These will be your major areas of expertise and satisfaction.

15. Avoid being defensive when confronted with conflict, but develop a soft and diplomatic response such as, *Tell me about your concerns; I am listening.* This approach usually defuses hostility and opens the door to better communication.

16. Strive to be an *enabler*, who is constantly trying to discover, enlist, and train Christians to serve the Lord and serve in church responsibilities (Ephesians 4:11–13).

17. Allow church leaders to make mistakes, and always affirm their good efforts. Most will never do as good a job the first time as you would have done.

18. Determine what kind of *rewards* it takes to motivate certain volunteers. Remember—*that which gets rewarded gets done.*

19. Take care of your own mental, emotional, spiritual, and physical health. You must set the pace since in ministry we control our own calendars most of the time.

20. If you work in a local church setting, make sure there is a balance between friends and acquaintances you have within the church and those you have outside your church.

Review Questions

1. Do you agree with the statement, "Developing good leadership is a lifelong growth experience"?

2. Why is it important to teach volunteer workers that "they do not work for or serve the pastor, the staff, the Sunday School director, or others"?

3. If you were a supervisor, how would you lead volunteer workers or staff members to develop their own vision for their ministries in the church?

4. What are some values that can come from having seasonal events for planning and motivation?

5. What are your preferences for giving recognition to volunteer workers and staff members you may be supervising?

For Further Reading

Dale, Robert D. *Sharing Ministry with Volunteer Leaders.* Nashville, TN: Convention Press, 1986.

Eldridge, Daryl, compiler. *The Teaching Ministry of the Church.* Nashville, TN: Broadman & Holman, 1999.

McDonough, Reginald M. *Keys to Effective Motivation.* Nashville, TN: Broadman Press, 1979.

Osmer, Richard Robert. *The Teaching Ministry of the Church.* Louisville, KY, Westminster John Knox Press, 2005.

Powers, Bruce P. *Christian Leadership.* Nashville, TN: Broadman Press, 1979.

Rainer, Thom, and Eric Geiger. *Simple Church.* Nashville, TN: Broadman Press, 2006.

Spooner, Bernard M., gen. ed. *Pastor, Staff, and Congregational Relationships: Through Servant Leadership and Quality Administration.* Coppell, TX: Christian Leadership Publishing, 2014.

Warren, Rick. *The Purpose Driven Life: What on Earth Am I Here For?* Grand Rapids, MI: Zondervan, 2002.

Wilson, Marlene. *How to Mobilize Church Volunteers.* Minneapolis, MN: Augsburg Publishing House, 1983.

Appendix 1

ADDITIONAL FACILITY CONSIDERATIONS FOR EDUCATION SPACE FOR PRESCHOOLERS AND CHILDREN

By Keith Crouch, AIA, NCARB

The following comments are provided by Keith Crouch, AIA, NCARB, director of church architecture for the Baptist General Convention of Texas. The comments address architectural and code-related items.

Classrooms for Sunday School

1. Commonly thirty-five square feet per preschooler and twenty-five square feet per grade school child will be used to determine the room capacity by church education specialists. Smaller church settings will use less. (However, building code officials will usually use twenty square feet per

189

person.) Please refer to http://texasbaptists.org/ministries/ church-administrative-resources/church-architecture for online FACTSheets for "Preschool Education Space" and "Children's Education Space" for more detailed information.

2. Square-foot factors and maximum room capacities are listed below. Not all rooms have to be the same size. Please refer to http://texasbaptists.org/ministries/church-administrative-resources/church-architecture for preschool and children.

Age Group	Space per child*	Recommended Capacity
Bed Babies	35 square feet per child	9 children per room
Toddlers	35 square feet per child	9 children per room
Two-Year-Olds	35 square feet per child	12 children per room
Three-Year-Olds	35 square feet per child	16 children per room
Four-Year-Olds	35 square feet per child	16 children per room
Five-Year-Olds	35 square feet per child	16 children per room
Grades 1–6	25 square feet per child	24 children per room

*In smaller church and alternative church settings, twenty-five square feet per preschooler may be acceptable.

3. Additionally it is preferable to use a room with a rectangular shape (like a three-by-five notecard) rather than a square room.

4. For all preschoolers and children grade three and under, the classrooms should be located on the ground floor, which is usually required by law and licensed daycare standards.

5. It is usually recommended that no classroom be narrower than twelve feet wide in either direction.

6. For child-care security reasons, we also recommend no closets in classrooms. The option is to use cabinets as shown in the floor plan diagrams in Appendix 2.

7. Visibility into the classroom is also preferable for child-care security purposes and church liability purposes. This can be achieved by a slender viewing window in the door to the classroom, a glass sidelight adjacent to the entrance door, or a separate window in the hallway wall (if permitted by code. In some cases the corridor wall is a fire-rated wall and limits the amount of openings for doors and viewing windows).

New and Smaller Churches

8. New church starts, mission churches, and smaller congregation churches are often challenged with lack of classroom space. Therefore many of the above mentioned guidelines are not achievable. Keep in mind some of the following:

    a. In smaller attendance settings, the preference would be more teaching units (two to three smaller rooms) for the preschool ages (bed babies and toddlers in one room and older preschool in another room) rather than one large room with a wide range of ages such as toddlers to five-year-olds.

b. Also in smaller attendance settings, it may be that twenty-five square feet per preschooler is used in lieu of thirty-five square feet. Also, twenty to twenty-five square feet per child may be used for the room capacity in the grade school classes.

Code Compliance

9. When planning a new building, or particularly before remodeling in an existing building, *a review by a licensed architect, licensed interior designer, or registered accessibility specialist* can help address code compliance with the classrooms.

10. Relative to room capacities for preschoolers and children, if there is a local building official, the official will usually use twenty square feet per person to determine the occupant load of a classroom, regardless of the age group, preschool through adults, using the room.

11. In many cases, churches will use their Sunday School rooms for other ministries as well. State licensed day care or federal Head Start programs may use thirty to thirty-five square feet person to determine the number of preschoolers or children allowed in a room. In some communities, the fire marshal may have additional restrictions on the number of children an indoor space will accommodate.

12. According to some state licensed day care standards (Department of Family and Protective Services Child-Care Center licensing, www.dfps.state.tx.us), the number of preschoolers or children allowed for enrollment depends on the number of drinking fountains, hand sinks, and toilets available. For every drinking fountain, hand sink, and toilet

available, you can enroll seventeen children (a 1:17 ratio), regardless of whether your rooms hold more children than that enrollment number.

13. There is a state building code, a state Texas accessibility standards, and Federal ADA (Americans with Disabilities Act) standard for people with handicaps. There is also a state licensed day care standard and building standards for some private weekday schools. However, *interpretation* of the codes and standards is left to discretion of the person with local jurisdiction. Therefore, we can make comments about how TDLR (Texas Department of Licensing and Regulation) intends compliance, but each church's local experience may vary.

14. In some communities, the state licensed day care authority requires every classroom to have an exterior fire exit door (usually to a playground area) in addition to the classroom door on the corridor. Also, in some communities the building official (if there is no day care, but may have Mother's Day Out) or state-licensed day care official will require operable windows at a specified window sill height as an alternative to an exterior door for emergency fire exit purposes.

Texas Accessibility Standards

15. Even if a classroom is used only for Sunday School, then the doors, countertops, and toilet rooms still must comply with the Texas Accessibility Standards (TAS) and Federal ADA. The TAS specifies the space around plumbing fixtures such as water closets and sinks, but also specifies mounting heights for those plumbing fixtures and mounting heights for all hand controls, such as towel dispensers, light switches, faucet handles, baby-changing stations, and so

on. This is a requirement for all new buildings *and* rooms or buildings that are altered by remodeling. If there are no alterations or remodeling, then an existing building is often *grandfathered* and does not have to come into current compliance until any remodeling changes are made. (Changing floor and wall finishes, painting, or replacing light fixtures or air conditioning is considered *refinishing* and not *remodeling*.)

16. Since there are numerous required measurements for toilet rooms adjacent to the classrooms, it is best to refer to the Architectural Barriers Texas Accessibility Standards online at www.tdlr.texas.gov/ab/abtas.htm. Be aware of the floor space around the water closets and sinks, the door swings, the knee clearance under the sinks, and the mounting heights for all hand controls, accessories, and light switches.

17. Depending on your governmental jurisdictions, a licensed professional, such as a licensed architect, a licensed interior designer, or a registered accessibility specialist can assist a church with handicap accessibility standards compliance.

18. In a general sense (refer to the standards in your locale), all doors need to be thirty-six inches wide, and all spaces (toilet rooms, hallway terminations, kitchens, offices, workrooms, resource rooms, foyers, and entrances) in your buildings need to allow for a wheelchair pivot, a five-foot (sixty-inch) circle. Also, all entrances and circulation inside the buildings must have compliant ramps that do not exceed the maximum slope and have the accompanying compliant handrails.

Features in Buildings

The following items are tips and suggestions for various features for buildings that accommodate preschoolers and children:

19. *Dutch doors* (doors divided into upper and lower halves) are sometimes used in preschool rooms. In some communities, the building official will not allow a Dutch door if it is located on a fire-rated corridor. Also, *if* a Dutch door is used, it is suggested that the upper half of the door have a one-inch gap at the bottom, covered with a soft-edged sweep to close the gap above the bottom half of the door. This safety feature avoids injury to preschoolers' fingers when closing the door halves.

20. For child-care security reasons, it is also recommended there be no closets in classrooms. The option is to use cabinets as shown in the floor plan diagrams (Appendix 2).

21. There is also a preference to recess the door in an alcove that enters into the classroom. The door still needs to swing out to the corridor. This is safer for preschoolers near the door. The door alcove is not a mandate by the building code, but it is a much safer condition when hallways are crowded or in an emergency fire situation. If no recessed alcove is used, then it is usually mandated by the building code and the Life Safety Code that the door cannot reduce the corridor or hallway to less than half its code-required width.

Appendix 2

CHILDREN'S ROOM DIAGRAMS

By B. J. Cranford, M. A. Religious Education

Anna Broussard, B. F. A. Communication Design

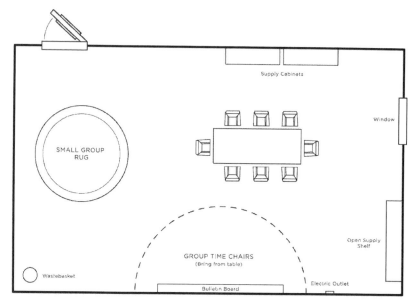

SMALLER CLASSROOM FOR CHILDREN

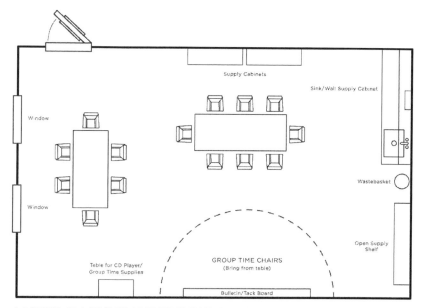

LARGER CLASS/DEPARTMENT FOR CHILDREN

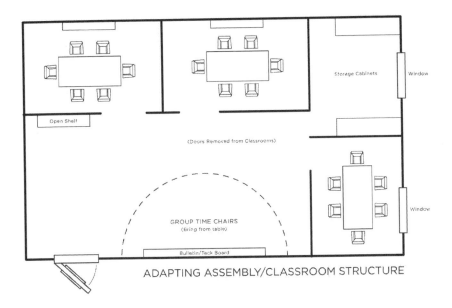

Storage Cabinets

Window

Open Shelf

(Doors Removed from Classrooms)

Window

GROUP TIME CHAIRS
(Bring from table)

Bulletin/Tack Board

ADAPTING ASSEMBLY/CLASSROOM STRUCTURE

Appendix 3

TEACHING PLANS

By Dennis Parrott, M.A. Religious Education

Chapter 1: Essential #1

1. Prepare a visual (markerboard, PowerPoint, or poster) of the book title. Begin the session with a brief overview of the book and a summary of the introduction.

2. Prepare a visual of the chapter title: "Value the All-Age Bible Teaching Approach of Sunday School and Small Groups." Lead participants to give their opinions in support of Sunday School and small groups. Then summarize the introductory paragraphs.

3. Prepare a visual of the terms *open groups* and *closed groups*. Read the two definitions found under the heading "Understanding Open Groups and Closed Groups." Invite participants to share experiences they have had with each type of group.

4. Refer to the chart titled "Small-Group Comparisons," and lead the group to look for the similarities and differences. (Provide the chart to participants who do not have a copy of the book.)

5. Refer to the ten best practices under the heading "Considering Some Best Practices." Prepare a visual of the best practices headings. Share information on each best practice. Then ask participants to select the two or three best practices that are most important to them and to share reasons for their selections. You may want to divide into groups of two for this activity.

6. Close with a summary of Arthur Flake's five principles for Sunday School growth.

Chapter 2: Essential #2

1. Prepare a visual for the chapter title "Ground Children's Ministry on Biblical and Theological Foundations." Give a brief lecture based on the introductory paragraphs related to faith development for children.

2. Prepare a visual for the question "Why Is Teaching Young Children Essential to the Mission of the Church?" Ask participants to share responses to this question. As seems needed, add to the class discussion information under the

heading "Why Is Teaching Young Children Essential to the Mission of the Church?"

3. Prepare slips of paper of the Bible references under the heading "The Old Testament Stresses God's Instructions about Teaching Young Children." Number the statements before distributing them to participants. Ask each member to read his or her slip of paper in correct numerical order. After the reading, invite participants to talk about the impact this instruction should make on their lives as parents and teachers.

4. Find a picture for display of Jesus with a group of children. Encourage participants to share their favorite stories of Jesus relating to and speaking about the importance of children. (Include material under the heading "Jesus Points out the Importance of Young Children" during this time of discussion.)

5. Summarize the material under the heading "Paul Points Out the Importance of Teaching Children in the Home," and ask participants why Paul considered it so important to teach children in the home.

6. Close with a brief lecture based on the material from the rest of this chapter.

Chapter 3: Essential #3

1. Prepare a visual for the chapter title "Understand the Context for Ministry for Today's Children and Their Families." Summarize the paragraphs at the beginning of this chapter to introduce this essential.

2. Prepare a visual similar to the following to use as you share the information related to the demographics for children. Emphasize the numbered items in your presentation.

Demographics

(1) Numbers of children—
(2) Changes in ethnicity—
(3) Poverty issues—
(4) Child care—
(5) Changing family structures—

3. Lead participants to discuss the impact on our churches of children's participation in educational institutions. Also, refer to the information on our children's educational achievements compared to other nations. Invite comments.

4. Ask participants whether they agree or disagree with the following statements related to the increased use of technology by children:

(1) It has resulted in adverse health outcomes.
(2) It has had a negative effect on children's creativity.
(3) It has hindered the development of social skills.

5. With regard to the section "Health and Physical Development," ask participants to give examples they have experienced with regard to the following:
(1) Obesity
(2) Attention deficit disorder, autism spectrum disorders, and mental health issues
(3) Serious health conditions
(4) Premature sexual activity, violence, substance abuse (Share the report from Barna quoted in the next to last paragraph

under the heading "Health and Physical Development,"
which begins, "Most of our young people. . . .")

6. Enlist a children's worker to provide information regarding
the security systems in place in your church, including the
use of background checks. Also ask the worker to share
information regarding the various weekday ministries to
children in your church. Instruct this worker to be prepared
to respond to the following question: *What priority is given
to children's ministry in this church?*

7. Present a brief lecture on the areas of connection between
the church and families of preschoolers based on the
material in the rest of this chapter.

Chapter 4: Essential #4

1. Prepare a visual of the chapter title. From the introductory
paragraph in this chapter, summarize the experience the
writer of this chapter had with his seven-year-old son.
Invite members to share similar experiences they have
had with their children or other children that support this
statement from paragraph two: "Young children are thinking
about God in ways that adults often are not aware." Read or
summarize the next two paragraphs, which begin, "Leaders
of children's ministries. . . ."

2. Ask participants how the teachings of Moses and Paul
and the early life of Jesus support the truth that children
can connect with God and grow spiritually. Support this
discussion with content under the heading "The Potential
for Spiritual Formation in Children Expressed in Scripture."

3. Present a brief lecture on the material related to using developmental science (see the information under the heading "Using Developmental Science to Get an Understanding of Spiritual Possibilities").

4. Summarize the information under the heading "Developmental Milestones in Middle Childhood." As you do, use the following questions for class discussion:
   a. What period in a child's life is included in middle childhood?
   b. What changes occur in a child's cognitive skills during this period?
   c. In what ways do sociological changes affect the child during middle childhood?
   d. What can be done to impact faith development during middle childhood?
   e. How is the development of a strong sense of self in this period of development revealed?
   f. What is the end stage of middle childhood?

5. Summarize the ministry practices for the three periods of middle childhood from the section "Ministry Practices as Children Grow."

6. Close by reading or summarizing the conclusion section.

Chapter 5: Essential #5

1. Prepare a visual to display the chapter title. Share the story about Wayne at the beginning of the chapter. Lead participants to discuss the importance of making such a commitment to children's ministry in their own lives.

2. Ask each participant to reflect on his or her role as a children's ministry leader and how that role should relate to the leadership role of the pastor. Say, "An admission of submission will make the next part of this discussion more important to the children's leader—enlisting the support of the pastor."

3. Write on the markerboard the three suggested ways to secure the support of the pastor, found under the heading "How to Secure the Support of Your Pastor." As each one is being discussed, lead participants to select at least one action they will take this next week.

4. Share the suggestions for gaining the support of other church staff, provided under the heading "How to Secure the Support of Other Staff Members." Ask, *How would you respond to such efforts directed toward you by other staff?*

5. Read this statement from the second paragraph under the heading "How to Secure the Support of Church Members": "One way to enlist the support of the church body for the children's ministry is to be visible to the church body." After reviewing the suggestions in this chapter about how to do this, invite participants to share additional ideas.

Chapter 6: Essential #6

1. Prepare a visual of the chapter title. Refer to and summarize the information about Christopher, Sarah, Andrew, and Psalm 139 in the introduction to the chapter.

2. Write "Know the Child" on the markerboard. Lead members to discuss each of the following statements as you write them on the board:
    a. Children are concrete thinkers.
    b. Children have short attention spans.

    Encourage the group to suggest implications of these characteristics. Summarize the information about visual, auditory, and kinesthetic learners. Refer to and invite discussion of question 1 under "Review Questions" at the end of the chapter.

3. Review with the group the information under "Organize for Teaching." Lead the group to evaluate their church's children's area by the information provided.

4. Refer to the information under the heading "Select Curriculum." Focus on the questions in the chart titled "Checklist of Preschool/Children Literature Characteristics." Lead the group to consider the literature they now use in relation to these questions. (Provide a copy of the questions to aid in discussion if participants do not have a copy of this book.)

5. Review with the group the information under "Guide Learning in Small Groups." Form groups of teachers for each age group listed, and ask each group to "walk through" the suggestions for small groups in their age group.

6. Then refer to the information under the subheads "Transition" and "Guide Worship in the Large Group." Review each element.

7. Invite comments about how the information presented in steps 5 and 6 would be helpful in the children's Bible teaching sessions in their church.

8. Close by reading or summarizing the information under "Conclusion."

Chapter 7: Essential #7

1. Prepare a visual to display the title of the chapter. Say, *Collaboration is essential if a church is to develop ministries and events that integrate unengaged families into the discipleship process.* From the information under the heading "Collaboration Is Essential," share the example of the church that lacked collaboration. Then summarize the information about millennials in the last two paragraphs under that heading. Allow participants to respond to these statements.

2. Read or summarize the information about synergy in the first paragraph under the heading "Collaboration Creates Synergy." Lead participants to respond to the last sentence in this paragraph. Share from this section the second example of the Jones family. Then say, *Note that there was a high level of collaboration with at least three different prongs of influence.* Use the information in the last paragraph of this section to identify those three prongs of influence.

3. Read the heading "But We Don't Have the Time or the Resources for All That Collaboration!" Allow participants to

respond to that statement before sharing the material in the first paragraph under that heading.

4. Be prepared to display the website of your church or to select a good example of a website to show participants during the discussion of websites and social media.

5. Summarize the information under the heading "Creating Ministries and Events That Serve as On-Ramps for Children and Their Families." Emphasize the suggestions for connecting families to the church through Vacation Bible School, weekday education programs, women's ministries, and seasonal programs and ministries. Lead participants to identify ideas that would work in their churches.

6. Close with the following quote from the last paragraph under the heading "Conclusion": "Millennial parents are not interested in being busier. They are looking for authentic relationships and opportunities to make a difference in their world."

Chapter 8: Essential #8

1. Prepare a visual of the chapter title. Enlist a person to tell the story of Hannah and another person to tell the story of Adoniram Judson from the information in the first four paragraphs. After these two presentations, enlist another person to read paragraphs five and six.

2. Share the story in the "Safety and Security" section about the lost child. Ask participants to respond to this question: *What*

could have been done to prevent this incident from happening at church? Refer to and summarize the suggestions in this section during the time of discussion.

3. From the final four paragraphs under the heading "Safety and Security," emphasize the information about drop-off and pickup policies. Ask participants to compare these ideas to their own procedures.

4. Display the five prevention techniques for dealing with sexual predators in the "Safety and Security" section. Explain and discuss each one. (Provide a copy of the prevention techniques if participants do not have this book.)

5. Refer to and summarize the information under the heading "Leadership Enlistment Policies." As you do, focus on the paragraph that begins, "Having enough teachers is a must," and especially this sentence in that paragraph: "For a top quality and safe environment for teaching, two adults (not married) need to be in the room when the first child arrives." Lead participants to consider reasons this guideline is important.

6. Close with a challenge for children's ministry workers to gain additional information about the parents and grandparents of their children.

Chapter 9: Essential #9

1. Prepare a visual for the title of the chapter. Share the information from the first paragraph. Ask participants to give reasons these statements are so true.

2. Refer to this statement from the first paragraph under the heading "How the Physical Environment Influences Learning/Competency": "Creating and implementing a learning environment means careful planning." If possible, lead participants to several children's rooms in your church as you consider the following questions from the second paragraph and the "First Impression Checklist":
   (1) Are the distracting features of the room eliminated?
   (2) Does the area smell clean?
   (3) Are the tables and chairs of the appropriate size?
   (4) Are the supplies neatly placed on shelves or countertops?
   (5) Are all visuals up-to-date with God-centered themes?
   (6) Is the room an adequate size?
   (7) Are the walls painted a soothing color?
   (8) Does the room meet the "Facility Safety Checklist"? (Refer to the list in this chapter or provide copies.)

3. Refer to and summarize the "Children's Education Space Guidelines" in this chapter. Lead participants to consider their own rooms in light of these guidelines. (Consider using the information as a checklist.)

4. Refer to and summarize the other concerns about the learning environment, such as security system, two adult teachers, and proper greeting procedures. Deal with the information under the heading "Furnishings and Equipment" that seems most needed for your situation. (Consider using the information as a checklist.)

5. Allow participants to express any concerns they may have regarding various church programs sharing space. Then refer to and read the information under the subhead

"Sharing Space." Lead the group to suggest ways to manage children's work on a limited budget.

6. Close with this statement (in a text box near the end of the chapter): "While providing resources for children's rooms is important, remember that the relationships with the teachers and children are most important. Children want to know whether their teachers are going to be there, whether their friends are going to be there, and what activities are planned."

Chapter 10: Essential #10

1. Prepare a visual of the chapter title. Ask participants to share their experiences with enlisting workers. Point out that everyone will agree that while this is one of the most difficult aspects of children's ministry work, it is also one of the greatest challenges as you seek to build God's team for your church.

2. Write Webster's definition of *volunteer* on the markerboard. (See the paragraph that begins, *"Webster's Dictionary..."* under the heading "Securing Body Builders.") Contrast that concept to this statement: "We need to change our focus from enlisting volunteers to enlisting committed Christ-followers." Invite comments.

3. Ask participants to respond to the question, *Where do you look for children's ministry body builders?* Share information under the heading "Securing Body Builders," during this discussion.

4. Distribute copies of the six points in this section related to organizing your ministry. Read aloud the paragraph after these six points, which begins, "Before you approach. . . ." Ask participants to suggest ways to balance aggressive worker recruitment with holding high standards for those who are willing to serve. After this discussion, review Jerry Stubblefield's enlistment process, which begins, "Before the meeting."

5. Review the section "Developing/Equipping Body Builders." As you share the examples of ministry training, ask participants to listen for how these fulfill the statement, "Ministry training should be both practical and convenient."

6. Summarize the information under the heading "Motivating Body Builders." Then ask participants to recall times they have been the recipients of motivation and ministry. Allow some to share their opinions regarding the importance of these two leadership factors.

Chapter 11: Essential #11

1. Prepare a visual of the chapter title. Refer to the first sentence under the heading "The Need for a Viable System of Communication," which reads, "The need for a viable system of effective communication with children, parents, teachers, and indeed throughout the whole congregation begins with *God's design for us to be in relationship with God and with each other.*" Present a brief lecture in support of this statement.

2. Invite participants to share examples of some of the tools they have used in effective communication. Add to this discussion various suggestions from the chapter, especially

the section "Tools to Consider for Effective Communication Systems."

3. As you summarize the material on "Communicating with Children," ask members to listen for the importance of relationships in the faith development of children and for the three kinds of messages that need to be directed to children. From the fourth paragraph under this heading, refer to the life phases suggested by Art Murphy. From the next paragraph, ask members to share ways that the *childhood* of children has changed. Invite participants to suggest some special events that can be used in communicating with children.

4. Summarize information under the heading "Communicating with Parents," as seems helpful. Ask participants to share experiences they have had in receiving communication from the church and from children's ministry leadership. Lecture briefly on the next section, which is on communicating with parents in crisis.

5. Summarize the information under the headings "Communicating with the Congregation" and "Communicating within the Church Organization." Encourage participants to listen for points that seem especially applicable to their situation. Invite comments about this and other things learned about this topic during this study.

Chapter 12: Essential #12

1. Prepare visuals of the chapter title and the chart related to worker potential at the beginning of the chapter. Refer to and read the following sentences from the third paragraph

of this chapter: "Developing good leadership is a lifelong growth experience. It requires careful attention to the process of leadership development and to being purposeful in the task at hand."

2. Read the Scriptures related to servant leadership under the heading "Jesus Demonstrated the Need for Servant Leadership." Enlist someone to read the four beliefs we need to teach Christian education workers, which are under the subhead "Motivate by Leading People to Have Beliefs and Convictions." Lead the group to discuss each one.

3. Refer to the subhead "Communicate a clear vision." Encourage participants to think of leaders who have modeled this well as you present this material.

4. Discuss different ways to involve people in vision development and planning. As you discuss the four groups of church participants listed under the subhead "Teach and develop a theology of culture and serving," encourage participants to determine in which group they would be placed.

5. Refer to the section "Seasonal Motivational Events for Key Leaders." Lead participants to share additional ideas for such events as you summarize this section.

6. Summarize the section "Giving Deserved Recognition." Lead participants to discuss the importance of giving deserved recognition.

7. Refer to and review Don Cannata's list of practical steps entitled "Succeeding in Church Leadership." (Provide a copy to participants who do not have this book.) Encourage participants to consider their ministry in light of these steps.

Notes

Note on the Foreword

1 "I Love to Tell the Story," words by Katherine Hankey.

Notes on chapter 1

2 Ed Stetzer and Eric Geiger, *Transformational Groups* (Nashville, TN: Broadman & Holman, 2014), 8.

3 James E. Coggin and Bernard M. Spooner, *You Can Reach People Now* (Nashville, TN: Broadman Press, 1981), 25–30.

4 Unless otherwise indicated, all Scripture quotations in chapter 1 are from the New International Version (1984 edition).

5 Gene Mims, *The Kingdom Focused Church: A Compelling Image of an Achievable Future* (Nashville, TN: Broadman & Holman, 2003), 130.

6 Mims, *The Kingdom Focused Church,* 141.

7 Ken Hemphill and Bill Taylor, *Ten Best Practices to Make Your Sunday School Work: Sunday School for a New Century* (Nashville, TN: LifeWay Press, 2001), 13.

8 Hemphill and Taylor, *Ten Best Practices,* 23–58.

9 Hemphill and Taylor, *Ten Best Practices,* 59–78.

10 Hemphill and Taylor, *Ten Best Practices,* 79–120.

11 Hemphill and Taylor, *Ten Best Practices,* 121—132.

[12] Hemphill and Taylor, *Ten Best Practices*, 133–154.
[13] Hemphill and Taylor, *Ten Best Practices*, 155–170.
[14] Hemphill and Taylor, *Ten Best Practices*, 171–180.
[15] Hemphill and Taylor, *Ten Best Practices*, 181–208.
[16] Hemphill and Taylor, *Ten Best Practices*, 209–222.
[17] Hemphill and Taylor, *Ten Best Practices*, 223–235.
[18] Bernard M. Spooner, gen. ed., *Christian Education Leadership: Making Disciples in the 21st Century Church* (Coppell, TX: Christian Leadership Publishing, 2012), 27.
[19] Arthur Flake, *Building a Standard Sunday School* (Nashville, TN: Sunday School Board of the Southern Baptist Convention, 1922).
[20] Flake, *Building a Standard Sunday School*, 21–39.

Notes on chapter 2

[21] Nathaniel Branden, *The Six Pillars of Self-Esteem* (New York: Bantam Books, 1994), xv
[22] Branden, *The Six Pillars of Self-Esteem*, 7.
[23] Joyce E. Bellous, Simone A. de Roos, and William Summey, *Children's Spirituality* (Eugene, OR: Cascade Books, 2004), 201.
[24] James W. Fowler, *Stages of Faith: The Psychology of Human Development and the Quest for Meaning* (New York: Harper Collins, 1981), 5.
[25] Unless otherwise indicated, all Scripture quotations in chapter 2 are from the New International Version (1984 edition).
[26] Rebecca Nye in *Children's Spirituality*, ed. Donald Ratcliff (Eugene, Oregon: Cascade Books, 2004), 91.
[27] http://divinity.yale.edu/gundry. Accessed 8/19/14.
[28] Judith Gundry-Volf in *The Child In Christian Thought*, ed. Marcia Bunge (Grand Rapids, MI: William B. Eerdmans Publishing Company, 2001), 38.
[29] See Gundry-Volf, *The Child In Christian Thought*, 43.

30 Gundry-Volf, *The Child In Christian Thought,* 43.
31 Andrew T. Lincoln, *Ephesians,* Word Biblical Commentary (Dallas, TX: Word Books, Publisher, 1990), 408.
32 Ratcliff, ed. *Children's Spirituality,* 49.

Notes on chapter 3

33 US Census Bureau, Current Population Reports. http:///www.childstats.gov/americanschildren/tables/pop2.asp.
34 "Child Population: Number of Children (in millions) ages 0–17 in the United States by Age, 1950–2013 and projected 2014–2050." ChildStats.gov. Forum on Child and Family Statistics. http://childstats.gov/americaschildren/tables/pop1.asp.
35 Kids Count Data Center: A Project of the Annie E. Casey Foundation, Child Population by Age Group. Http://datacenter.kidscount.org/data/tables/101-child-population. Accessed 8/28/14.
36 "Family Structure and Children's Living Arrangements," ChildStats.gov. http://www.childstats.gov/americanschildren/famsoc1.asp. Accessed 8/15/2014.
37 "Three Major Faith and Culture Trends for 2014," Barna Group. https://www.barna.org/barna-update/culture/652-3-vocational-trends-for-20143.U6iT414tM8M.
38 "American Students Fall in International Academic Tests, Chinese Lead the Pack," *U.S. News and World Report,* December 3, 2013. www.usnews.com/news/articles/2013/12/03/american-students-fall-in-internationall-academic-tests-chinese-lead-the-pack.
39 "Electronic Media Associated with Poorer Well-being in Children," *ScienceDaily.* http://www.sciencedaily.com/releases/2014/03/14031893918.htm. Accessed 8/28/14.
40 2011/2012 National Survey of Children's Health, Indicator 6.10c. http://childhealthdata.org/browse/survey/results.

[41] Kyung Kee Kim, "The Creativity Crisis: The Decrease in Creative Thinking Scores on the Torrance Tests of Creative Thinking," *Creativity Research Journal*, no. 23 (4) (2011): 285.

[42] Kyung Kee Kim, "The Creativity Crisis," 293.

[43] Valerie Strauss, "Is Technology Sapping Children's Creativity?" The Answer Sheet, blog post at http://www.washingtonpost.com/blogs/answer-sheet/post/is-technology-sapping-childrens-creativity/2012/09/12/10c63c7e-fced-11e1-a31e-804fccb658f9_blog.html. Accessed 8/28/14.

[44] "America's Children: Key National Indicators of Well-Being, 2013." ChildStats.gov. Forum on Child and Family Statistics. http://www.childstats.gov/americanschildren/glance.asp.

[45] "2011/2012 National Survey of Children's Health," Indicator 1.4a.

[46] "Obesity Rates Climbing Worldwide, Most Comprehensive Global Study to Date Shows," *ScienceDaily*. http://www.sciencedaily.com/releases/2014/05/140528204215.htm. Accessed 8/28/14.

[47] "Children's Mental Health—New Report," Centers for Disease Control and Prevention, www.cdc.gov/features/childrensmentalhealth/. Accessed 8/28/14.

[48] "Middle School Youth as Young as 12 Engaging in Risky Sexual Activity," *ScienceDaily*, http://www.sciencedaily.com/releases/2009/04/090408145354.htm. Accessed 9/26/14.

[49] George Barna, *Transforming Children into Spiritual Champions* (Ventura, CA: Regal Books, 2003), 26.

[50] George Barna, *Transforming Children into Spiritual Champions*, 39–40.

[51] George Barna, *Transforming Children into Spiritual Champions*, 40–41.

[52] "Fact2000 Study, Faith Communities Today, The Basic Demographic Profile of Respondents," http://faithcommunitiestoday.org/basic-demographic-profile-respondents. Accessed 8/28/14.

53 "FACTS on Growth, Worship, Websites, Conflict Affect Growth in Congregations," http://faithcommunitiestoday.org/worship-websites-conflict-affect-growth-congregations. Accessed 8/28/14.

54 "Summary Research Report of a New Decade of Megachurches," Hartford Institute for Religion Research, http://hirr.hartsem.edu/megachurch/megachurch-2011-summary-report-htm. Accessed 12/29/2011.

55 "Does Having Children Make Parents More Active Churchgoers?" Barna Group, https://www.barna.org/barna-update/family-kids/391-does-having-children-make-parents-more-active-churchgoers#.U-04ukhzoaZ.

56 George Barna, *Transforming Children into Spiritual Champions*, 14.

57 George Barna, *Transforming Children into Spiritual Champions*, 98.

58 Janice Haywood, *Enduring Connections: Creating a Preschool and Children's Ministry* (St. Louis, MO: Chalice Press, 2007), 1.

59 Janice Haywood, *Enduring Connections*, 6.

60 Janice Haywood, *Enduring Connections*, 24.

61 Michael J. Anthony, ed., *Perspectives on Children's Spiritual Formation* (Nashville: B&H Academic, 2006), 36–41.

Notes on chapter 4

62 Joel B. Green, *The Gospel of Luke* (Grand Rapids, MI: Wm. B. Eerdmans, 1997), 154.

63 James W. Fowler, *Stages of Faith: The Psychology of Human Development and the Quest for Meaning* (New York: HarperCollins, 1981).

64 E.C. Roehlkepartain, P.E. King, L. Wagener, and P.L. Benson, eds., *The Handbook of Spiritual Development in Childhood and*

Adolescence (Thousand Oaks, CA: Sage Publications, 2006), 181–182.

[65] J. Piaget, "Piaget's Theory," in P. Mussen, ed. *Charmichel's Manual of Child Psychology*, 3rd edition, vol. 1 (New York: John Wiley and Sons, 1970).

[66] E. H. Erickson, *Childhood and Society*, 2nd ed. (New York: Norton, 1963).

Notes on chapter 5

[67] Thom Rainer, *Surprising Insights from the Unchurched* (Grand Rapids, MI: Zondervan, 2001).

[68] E. Selzer, "Effectiveness of a Seminary's Training and Mentoring Program and Subsequent Job Satisfaction of Its Graduates," *Journal of Research on Christian Education*, no. 17 (2008):25–53.

[69] R. Pope, *The Prevailing Church* (Chicago: Moody Press, 2002).

[70] George Barna, *The State of the Church* (Ventura, CA: Issachar Resources, 2002).

[71] B. Bass, ed., *Leadership in Congregations* (Herndon, VA: The Alban Institute, 2007).

[72] R. Couch, *The Ministry of Childhood Education*, 3rd ed. (Nashville, TN: LifeWay Christian, 2000).

[73] George Barna, ed., *Leaders on Leadership: Wisdom, Advice and Encouragement on the Art of Leading God's People* (Ventura, CA: Regal Books, 1997).

[74] Couch, *The Ministry of Childhood Education*.

[75] Gene Mims, *The Kingdom Focused Church* (Nashville, TN: Broadman & Holman Publishers, 2003).

[76] Diana R. Garland, *Family Ministry: a Comprehensive Guide* (Downers Grove, IL: InterVarsity Press, 2012).

77 E. Johnson and B. Bower, *Building a Great Children's Ministry* (Nashville, TN: Abingdon Press, 1992).

78 Garland, *Family Ministry.*

79 Johnson and Bower, *Building a Great Children's Ministry.*

80 Couch, *The Ministry of Childhood Education.*

Notes on chapter 6

81 For a description of children's developmental characteristics, see Michelle Anthony, "Childhood Education" in Michael J. Anthony, ed., *Introducing Christian Education: Foundations for the Twenty-first Century* (Grand Rapids, MI: Baker Academic, 2001), 211–214.

82 Norma Hedin, "Teaching Children" in Daryl Eldridge, *The Teaching Ministry of the Church* (Nashville, TN: Broadman & Holman Publishers, 1995), 228–231.

83 Hedin, "Teaching Children," 230–231.

84 Anne Tonks, *Toward 2000: Leading Children in Sunday School* (Nashville, TN: Convention Press, 1985), 19.

85 Eugene Chamberlain and Robert Fulbright, *Children's Sunday School Work* (Nashville, TN: Convention Press, 1969), 30.

86 Tonks, *Toward 2000: Leading Children in Sunday School*, 27.

87 Paula Stringer and James Hargrave, *Crayons, Computers and Kids* (Nashville, TN: Convention Press, 1996).

88 *How to Evaluate Literature for Preschoolers and Children*, Bible Study/Discipleship Center, Baptist General Convention of Texas.

89 *How to Evaluate Literature for Preschoolers and Children.*

90 Steve Parr, *Sunday School That Really Works* (Grand Rapids, MI: Kregel Publications, 2010), 86.

Notes on chapter 7

91 Ed Stetzer, Richie Stanley, and Jason Hayes, *Lost and Found: The Younger Unchurched and the Churches that Reach Them*, (Nashville: B & H Publishing Group, 2009), 23.

92 Andrew Hess and Glenn T. Stanton, "Millennial Faith Participation and Retention," http://www.focusonthefamily.com/about_us/focus-findings/religion-and-culture/millennial-retention.aspx. Accessed 8/28/14.

93 Pew Research Study, "Growth of the NonReligious", July 2, 2013. http://www.pewforum.org/2013/07/02/growth-of-the-nonreligious-many-say-trend-is-bad-for-american-society/. Accessed 8/28/14.

94 George Barna, "5 Reasons Millennials Stay Connected to Church," https://www.barna.org/barna-update/millennials/635-5-reasons-millennials-stay-connected-to-church#.U6dR8Rb7WfQ. Accessed 8/28/14.

95 www.merriam-webster.com/dictionary/synergy. Accessed 8/28/14.

96 Thom S. Rainer and Eric Geiger, *Simple Church* (Nashville: B & H Publishing Group, 2006), 14.

97 Thom S. Rainer and Eric Geiger, *The Millennials: Connecting to America's Largest Generation* (Nashville: B & H Publishing Group, 2011), 103.

98 Jeff Fromm and Christie Garton, *Marketing to Millennials* (New York: American Management Association, 2013), 75.

99 Paul Taylor, *The Next America* (New York: Perseus Books, 2014), 139.

100 George Barna, "How Technology is Changing Millennial Faith" https://www.barna.org/barna-update/millennials/640-how-technology-is-changing-millennial-faith#.U6dTmxb7WfQ. Accessed 6/4/14.

101 The Millennial Impact Executive Summary, http://www.the-millennialimpact.com/mcon14-downloadreport, 5. Accessed 8/28/14.

102 Millennial Impact Executive Summary.

103 Adam Lella, "Why are Millennials so Mobile?" (Feb. 23, 2014) http://www.washingtonpost.com/business/capitalbusiness/why-are-millennials-so-mobile/2014/02/21/b3893a60-9819-11e3-8461-8a24c7bf0653_story.html. Accessed 8/28/14.

104 Jerry Wooley, "Making Continued Connections through VBS" (April 1, 2014) http://www.lifeway.com/kidsministry/2014/04/01/making-continued-connections-through-vbs/. Accessed 8/28/14.

105 Wooley, "Making Continued Connections through VBS."

106 See http://www.upward.org. Accessed 10/2/14.

107 Barna Group, "The Spirituality of Moms outpaces Dads" (May 7, 2007) https://www.barna.org/barna-update/family-kids/104-the-spirituality-of-moms-outpaces-that-of-dads#.U6dUlRb7WfQ. Accessed 6/15/14.

108 Stetzer, Stanley, and Hayes, *Lost and Found*, 144.

Notes on chapter 8

109 All Scripture quotations in this chapter are taken from the Holman Christian Standard Bible (HCSB) unless otherwise stated.

110 Beverly Wingo Thompson, *Luther Rice, Believer in Tomorrow* (Nashville: Broadman Press, 1967), 122.

111 MinistrySafe.com, directed by Gregory Love and Kimberlee Norris, sexual abuse lawyers who practice law through Love &

Norris and are directors of *MinistrySafe*, an entity that designs and implements sexual abuse safety systems for church and parachurch ministries.

Notes on chapter 9

[112] D. Guerin (2003), "Design for Development: The Importance of Children's Environments," *Implications*. http://www.informedesign.org/_news/Children01_02.pdf. Accessed 10/3/14.

[113] A. V. Fisher, K. E. Godwin, and H. Seltman, "Visual Environment, Attention Allocation, and Learning in Young Children When Too Much of a Good Thing May Be Bad," *Psychological Science (2014).*

[114] J. Smith, *Essentials for Excellence: Connecting Children's Sunday School to Life.* Nashville, TN: LifeWay Press, 2003).

[115] Kaiser Family Foundation, Generation M2: Media in the Lives of 8- to 18-Year-Olds, 2010.

[116] http://pediatrics.aappublications.org/content/132/5/958.full?sid=0d8dc450-d8e0-4d1f-98e7-35327be00615. Accessed 10/3/14.

[117] http://www.huffingtonpost.com/cris-rowan/technology-children-negative-impact_b_3343245.html?utm_hp_ref=email_share. Accessed 10/3/14.

[118] "Technology and Interactive Media as Tools in Early Childhood Programs Serving Children from Birth through Age 8" http://www.naeyc.org/content/technology-and-young-children. Accessed 10/3/14.

[119] P. Stringer and J. Hargrave, *Crayons, Computers & Kids* (Nashville, TN: Convention Press, 1996).

[120] K. Winter and R. Gyuse, *Creating Quality School-Age Child Care* (New York: Local Initiatives Support Corporation, 2011).

121 *Children's Spaces at Church.* Childhood Ministry of Baptist State Convention of North Carolina. http://www.ncbaptist.org/fileadmin/ministries/children/resources/2013/pdfs/files/childrens-space-church.pdf. Accessed 10/3/14.

122 *Children's Spaces at Church.*

123 *Children's Spaces at Church.*

124 Adapted from A. M. Gordon, K. W. Browne, and D. W. Hewes, *Beginnings & Beyond: Foundations in Early Childhood Education* (Albany, NY: Delmar Publishers, 1993).

125 *Children's Spaces at Church.*

Notes on chapter 10

126 All Scripture quotations in this chapter are taken from the Holman Christian Standard Bible (HCSB) unless otherwise stated.

127 The New Lexicon Webster's Dictionary of the English Language (1987), s.v. "Volunteer."

128 http://www.bls.gov/news.release/volun.toc.htm. Accessed 9/1/14.

129 Tina Houser, *Building Children's Ministry* (Nashville: Thomas Nelson, 2008), 16.

130 The Guide One Center for Risk Management, *The Missing Ministry: Safety, Risk Management, and Protecting Your Church* (Loveland, CO: Group Publishing, 2008), 124–125.

131 Carolyn C. Brown, *Developing Christian Education in the Smaller Church* (Nashville: Abingdon, 1982), 47.

132 Scottie May and others, *Children Matter: Celebrating Their Place in the Church, Family, and Community* (Grand Rapids, MI: Eerdmans, 2005), 346.

133 Jerry Stubblefield, "How to Staff and Motivate," in Bruce P. Powers, *Christian Education Handbook* (Nashville: Broadman and Holman, 1996), 91–93.

134 John Maxwell, *Developing the Leader within You* (Nashville: Thomas Nelson, 1993), 121–122.

135 Lawrence Richards, *New International Encyclopedia of Bible Words* (Grand Rapids, MI: Zondervan, 1991), 146.

136 Adapted from Cindy Lumpkin and Tommy Sanders, *Children Sunday School for a New Century* (Nashville: LifeWay Press, 1999), 46–47.

137 Names are changed.

Notes on chapter 11

138 Michael J. Anthony and James Estep, Jr., eds., "Decision Making and Communication within the Organization," in *Management Essentials for Christian Ministries,* (Nashville, TN: Broadman & Holman Publishers, 2005), 239.

139 Craig Jutila, *The Growing Leader: Healthy Essentials for Children's Ministry* (Loveland, CO: Group Publishing, 2004), 103.

140 Janice Haywood, *Enduring Connections: Creating a Preschool and Children's Ministry* (Danvers, MA: Chalice Press, 2007), 62.

141 Jim Wideman, *Stretch: Structuring Your Ministry for Growth* (Murfreesboro, TN: An Infuse Publication, 2011), 124.

142 Craig Jutila, "The 21st-Century Digital Age" in *Children's Ministry in the 21st Century,* eds. Heather Dunn, Amber Van Schooneveld, and Anne Marie Rozum (Loveland, CO: Group Publishing, 2007), 111.

143 Scottie May, Beth Posterski, Catherine Stonehouse, and Linda Cannell, *Children Matter: Celebrating Their Place in the Church, Family, and Community* (Grand Rapids, MI: Wm. B. Eerdmans Publishing Co., 2005), 3.

144 Michael Anthony, ed., *Perspectives on Children's Spiritual Formation* (Nashville, TN: Broadman & Holman Publishers, 2006), 34.

145 www.Tru.DavidCCook.com. Accessed 10/6/14.

146 Craig Jutila, "The 21st-Century Digital Age" in *Children's Ministry in the 21st Century,* 184.

147 Wideman, *Stretch,* 126.

148 Catherine Stonehouse, *Joining Children on the Spiritual Journey: Nurturing a Life of Faith* (Grand Rapids, MI: BridgePoint Book, 1998), 63.

149 Tedd Tripp, *Shepherding a Child's Heart* (Wapwallopen, PA: Shepherd Press, 1995), 76.

150 Stonehouse, *Joining Children on the Spiritual Journey,* 67.

151 May, Posterski, Stonehouse, and Cannell, *Children Matter,* 165.

152 Sue Miller and David Staal, *Making Your Children's Ministry the Best Hour of Every Kid's Week* (Grand Rapids, MI: Zondervan, 2004), 66.

153 Art Murphy, *The Faith of a Child: A Step-by-Step Guide to Salvation for Your Child* (Chicago, IL: Moody Publishers, 2000), 62.

154 Julie A. Gorman, "Children and Developmentalism," in *Nurture That is Christian,* eds. James C. Wilhoit and John M. Dettoni (Grand Rapids, MI: BridgePoint Books, 1995), 156.

155 Rick Chromey, "The Times They Are a-Changin'" in *Children's Ministry in the 21st Century,* eds. Heather Dunn, Amber Van Schooneveld, and Anne Marie Rozum (Loveland, CO: Group Publishing, 2007), 13.

156 Miller and Staal, *Making Your Children's Ministry the Best Hour of Every Kid's Week,* 75.

157 Haywood, *Enduring Connections,* 63.

158 Cheryl Dunlop, *Follow Me as I Follow Christ: A Guide for Teaching Children in a Church Setting* (Chicago, IL: Moody Press, 2000), 140.

159 Haywood, *Enduring Connections,* 63.

160 Reggie Joiner, *Think Orange: Imagine the Impact when Church and Family Collide.* (Colorado Springs, CO: David C. Cook, 2009), 86.

[161] Catherine Stonehouse and Scottie May, *Listening to Children on the Spiritual Journey: Guidance for Those Who Teach and Nurture* (Grand Rapids, MI: Baker Academic, 2010), 138.

[162] Ben Freudenburg and Rick Lawrence, *The Family-Friendly Church* (Loveland, CO: 1998), 100.

[163] Stonehouse, *Joining Children on the Spiritual Journey,* 65.

[164] Wideman, *Stretch,* 123.

[165] Larry Fowler, *Rock Solid Volunteers* (Ventura, CA: Regal, 2010), 80.

[166] Miller and Staal, *Making Your Children's Ministry the Best Hour of Every Kid's Week,* 120–129.

[167] Fowler, *Rock Solid Volunteers,* 104.

[168] Marlene Wilson, *Volunteer Encouragement, Evaluation, and Accountability* (Loveland, CO: Group Publishing, 2004), 11.

[169] Christine Yount, *Awesome Volunteers* (Loveland, CO: Group Publishing, 1998), 51.

[170] Yount, *Awesome Volunteers,* 57.

[171] Wideman, *Stretch,* 124.

[172] Anthony and Estep, *Management Essentials for Christian Ministries,* 239.

[173] Wideman, *Stretch,* 122. Wilson, *Volunteer Encouragement, Evaluation, and Accountability,* 12.

[174] Haywood, *Enduring Connections,* 66.

[175] Haywood, *Enduring Connections,* 66.

[176] Haywood, *Enduring Connections,* 67.

[177] Wideman, *Stretch,* 121.

[178] Wideman, *Stretch,* 127.

[179] Anthony and Estep, *Management Essentials for Christian Ministries,* 270.

[180] Yount, *Awesome Volunteers,* 51.

[181] Wilson, *Volunteer Encouragement, Evaluation, and Accountability,* 39.

Notes on chapter 12

182 Reginald M. McDonough, *Keys to Effective Motivation* (Nashville, TN: Broadman Press, 1979), 79–82.

183 Adapted from McDonough, *Keys to Effective Motivation*, 79–82.

184 Unless otherwise indicated, all Scripture quotations in chapter 12 are from the New International Version (1984 edition).

185 For a helpful brief approach to Baptist beliefs, see Bernard M. Spooner, gen. ed., *Handbook for Baptists: What Every Baptist (New or Longtime) Should Know* (Coppell, TX: Christian Leadership Publishing, 2013).

186 Rick Warren, *The Purpose Driven Church: Growth Without Compromising Your Message & Mission* (Grand Rapids, MI: Zondervan Publishing House, 1995), 307–392.

Made in the USA
Charleston, SC
29 July 2015